DESKTOP SUPPORT CRASH COURSE

TECHNICAL PROBLEM SOLVING AND NETWORK TROUBLESHOOTING

4 BOOKS IN 1

BOOK 1
DESKTOP SUPPORT ESSENTIALS: A BEGINNER'S GUIDE TO TROUBLESHOOTING

BOOK 2
MASTERING NETWORK BASICS: FUNDAMENTAL TECHNIQUES FOR DESKTOP SUPPORT

BOOK 3
ADVANCED DESKTOP SUPPORT STRATEGIES: DEEP DIVE INTO SYSTEM DIAGNOSTICS

BOOK 4
EXPERT-LEVEL NETWORK TROUBLESHOOTING: PRO TIPS FOR RESOLVING COMPLEX ISSUES

ROB BOTWRIGHT

Published by Rob Botwright
Library of Congress Cataloging-in-Publication Data
ISBN 978-1-83938-740-1
Cover design by Rizzo

Disclaimer

The contents of this book are based on extensive research and the best available historical sources. However, the author and publisher make no claims, promises, or guarantees about the accuracy, completeness, or adequacy of the information contained herein. The information in this book is provided on an "as is" basis, and the author and publisher disclaim any and all liability for any errors, omissions, or inaccuracies in the information or for any actions taken in reliance on such information. The opinions and views expressed in this book are those of the author and do not necessarily reflect the official policy or position of any organization or individual mentioned in this book. Any reference to specific people, places, or events is intended only to provide historical context and is not intended to defame or malign any group, individual, or entity. The information in this book is intended for educational and entertainment purposes only. It is not intended to be a substitute for professional advice or judgment. Readers are encouraged to conduct their own research and to seek professional advice where appropriate. Every effort has been made to obtain necessary permissions and acknowledgments for all images and other copyrighted material used in this book. Any errors or omissions in this regard are unintentional, and the author and publisher will correct them in future editions.

BOOK 1 - DESKTOP SUPPORT ESSENTIALS: A BEGINNER'S GUIDE TO TROUBLESHOOTING

BOOK 2 - MASTERING NETWORK BASICS: FUNDAMENTAL TECHNIQUES FOR DESKTOP SUPPORT

BOOK 3 - ADVANCED DESKTOP SUPPORT STRATEGIES: DEEP DIVE INTO SYSTEM DIAGNOSTICS

BOOK 4 - EXPERT-LEVEL NETWORK TROUBLESHOOTING: PRO TIPS FOR RESOLVING COMPLEX ISSUES

Introduction

Welcome to the "Desktop Support Crash Course: Technical Problem Solving And Network Troubleshooting" bundle, a comprehensive collection designed to equip you with the essential skills and knowledge needed to excel in desktop support and network troubleshooting roles. Whether you're just starting your journey in IT support or looking to advance your existing skills, this bundle offers a structured learning path that covers everything from the fundamentals to expert-level techniques.

Book 1, "Desktop Support Essentials: A Beginner's Guide to Troubleshooting," serves as your entry point into the world of desktop support. This book provides a solid foundation in troubleshooting principles, teaching you how to identify and resolve common hardware and software issues encountered in desktop environments. With step-by-step instructions and practical examples, you'll learn how to diagnose problems, troubleshoot operating system issues, and communicate effectively with end-users.

Building on this foundation, Book 2, "Mastering Network Basics: Fundamental Techniques for Desktop Support," explores the fundamentals of networking essential for desktop support professionals. From understanding IP addressing and subnetting to configuring network devices and protocols, this book covers the essential networking concepts needed to troubleshoot basic network connectivity issues. By the end of this book, you'll have a solid understanding of network fundamentals and be ready to tackle common network problems with confidence.

Book 3, "Advanced Desktop Support Strategies: Deep Dive into System Diagnostics," takes your troubleshooting skills to the next level by diving deep into system diagnostics and advanced troubleshooting techniques. You'll learn how to analyze system logs, perform performance tuning, and troubleshoot complex hardware and software issues encountered in desktop environments. With real-world scenarios and practical examples, this book prepares you to handle challenging desktop support scenarios with ease.

Finally, Book 4, "Expert-Level Network Troubleshooting: Pro Tips for Resolving Complex Issues," focuses on advanced network troubleshooting strategies and techniques. From packet analysis to protocol analysis and network security, this book equips you with the knowledge and tools needed to diagnose and resolve complex network issues efficiently. With expert tips and best practices, you'll learn how to tackle even the most challenging network problems like a seasoned professional.

Whether you're a novice looking to break into the field of desktop support or an experienced professional seeking to enhance your skills, the "Desktop Support Crash Course" bundle has something for everyone. Join us on this learning journey as we explore the essentials of desktop support and network troubleshooting, from beginner to expert level.

BOOK 1
DESKTOP SUPPORT ESSENTIALS
A BEGINNER'S GUIDE TO TROUBLESHOOTING

ROB BOTWRIGHT

Chapter 1: Introduction to Desktop Support

Desktop Support Technicians play a crucial role in ensuring the smooth functioning of an organization's IT infrastructure. They are the frontline responders to various technical issues encountered by end-users, ranging from hardware malfunctions to software glitches. These technicians possess a diverse skill set encompassing hardware troubleshooting, software installation, network configurations, and user support. They serve as the bridge between technology and end-users, translating complex technical jargon into understandable terms for non-technical staff.

One of the primary responsibilities of Desktop Support Technicians is to diagnose and resolve hardware issues encountered by users. Whether it's a malfunctioning keyboard, a faulty monitor, or a malfunctioning printer, technicians must quickly identify the root cause of the problem and provide an effective solution. This often involves conducting hardware diagnostics, testing components, and, if necessary, replacing defective parts. For instance, if a user reports a non-responsive mouse, technicians may use diagnostic tools to check the connection, replace the batteries, or swap the mouse with a functioning one.

In addition to hardware troubleshooting, Desktop Support Technicians are also tasked with software installation and configuration. They are responsible for deploying new software applications across the organization, ensuring compatibility with existing systems, and configuring settings according to user requirements. This may involve using command-line interface (CLI) commands or graphical user interface (GUI) tools to install software packages, configure settings, and perform necessary updates. For example, technicians may deploy software updates using package management tools like apt-get or yum in Linux environments, or PowerShell commands in Windows environments.

Furthermore, Desktop Support Technicians are entrusted with maintaining and managing the organization's network infrastructure. They are responsible for setting up network connections, configuring routers and switches, and troubleshooting network-related issues. This includes ensuring proper IP addressing, subnetting, and DNS configurations to facilitate seamless communication between devices. Technicians may use CLI commands such as ipconfig, ifconfig, or ping to troubleshoot network connectivity problems, identify IP conflicts, or diagnose DNS resolution issues.

Moreover, Desktop Support Technicians serve as the first point of contact for end-users seeking assistance with various IT-related issues. They provide technical support via phone, email, or in-person interactions, guiding users through troubleshooting steps and resolving issues in a timely manner. Effective communication skills are essential in this role, as technicians must communicate technical information clearly and concisely to users with varying levels of technical expertise.

Another critical aspect of the Desktop Support Technician's role is ensuring the security of the organization's IT infrastructure. They are responsible for implementing security measures such as antivirus software, firewalls, and access controls to protect against cyber threats and unauthorized access. This includes educating users about security best practices, conducting security audits, and enforcing compliance with IT security policies. Technicians may use CLI commands to configure firewall rules, update antivirus definitions, or perform security scans to detect and mitigate potential vulnerabilities.

Furthermore, Desktop Support Technicians play a vital role in data backup and recovery efforts. They are responsible for implementing backup solutions to safeguard critical data against loss or corruption and facilitating data recovery in the event of a disaster. This may involve configuring backup schedules, monitoring backup jobs, and conducting regular data integrity checks. In the event of data loss or system failure, technicians must quickly restore data from backups using appropriate recovery procedures.

Additionally, Desktop Support Technicians are involved in user training and documentation efforts to promote IT literacy and self-service capabilities among end-users. They create user manuals, knowledge base articles, and instructional materials to assist users in troubleshooting common issues independently. This proactive approach not only empowers users to resolve minor technical issues on their own but also reduces the workload on support staff, allowing them to focus on more complex tasks.

In summary, Desktop Support Technicians play a multifaceted role in ensuring the efficient operation of an organization's IT environment. From diagnosing hardware issues to providing software support, configuring network infrastructure, ensuring cybersecurity, and facilitating user training, these technicians are indispensable members of the IT team. Their expertise and dedication contribute to the overall productivity, efficiency, and security of the organization's IT infrastructure.

Customer service skills are paramount in today's business landscape, transcending industries and organizational structures. These skills form the cornerstone of successful interactions between businesses and their customers, shaping the overall perception of the brand and fostering long-term relationships. In a world where consumer expectations continue to evolve rapidly, mastering customer service skills has become a critical priority for businesses seeking to differentiate themselves in competitive markets and cultivate customer loyalty.

Effective communication lies at the heart of exceptional customer service. Whether interacting with customers face-to-face, over the phone, or through digital channels, the ability to convey information clearly, empathetically, and courteously is essential. Active listening, a fundamental component of communication, enables service representatives to understand customer needs, concerns, and preferences accurately. By listening attentively and asking probing questions, representatives can gather pertinent information to provide tailored solutions and personalized assistance. This fosters a sense of trust and rapport, signaling to customers that their concerns are valued and understood.

Empathy is another key attribute of exemplary customer service. Empathetic service representatives demonstrate genuine concern for customers' well-being and strive to understand their perspectives and emotions. By placing themselves in the customer's shoes and acknowledging their feelings, representatives can establish a deeper connection and build rapport. Empathy enables representatives to handle challenging situations with sensitivity and tact, defusing tensions and de-escalating conflicts effectively. When customers feel heard, understood, and cared for, they are more likely to develop a positive perception of the brand and remain loyal in the long run.

Moreover, effective problem-solving skills are indispensable in the realm of customer service. Customers often turn to businesses seeking solutions to issues or challenges they encounter. Service representatives must possess the analytical acumen and resourcefulness to identify root causes, evaluate alternatives, and implement viable solutions promptly. This may involve troubleshooting technical problems, resolving billing discrepancies, or addressing product-related concerns. By demonstrating proficiency in problem-solving, representatives instill confidence in customers and reaffirm the organization's commitment to delivering value and satisfaction.

In addition to communication, empathy, and problem-solving, adaptability is a crucial attribute in the realm of customer service. The modern business landscape is dynamic and ever-changing, characterized by evolving customer preferences, emerging technologies, and shifting market trends. Service representatives must possess the flexibility and agility to navigate these changes adeptly, adjusting their approach and strategies to meet evolving customer needs. Whether integrating new communication channels, embracing innovative technologies, or adapting workflows to accommodate changing demand patterns, adaptability enables representatives to stay responsive and relevant in a dynamic environment.

Furthermore, professionalism is a cornerstone of exceptional customer service. Professionalism encompasses a range of attributes, including reliability, integrity, and accountability. Service representatives must conduct themselves with professionalism at all times, adhering to ethical standards, company policies, and industry regulations. This entails honoring commitments, maintaining confidentiality, and handling sensitive information with discretion and integrity. Professionalism fosters trust and credibility, reinforcing the organization's reputation and instilling confidence in customers.

Additionally, patience and resilience are essential virtues in the field of customer service. Dealing with diverse customer personalities, resolving complex issues, and managing high-stress situations can be inherently challenging. Service representatives must remain composed, patient, and resilient in the face of adversity, maintaining a positive attitude and persevering through obstacles. By demonstrating patience and resilience, representatives can effectively manage customer expectations, diffuse tension, and navigate difficult interactions with professionalism and grace.

Moreover, continuous learning and development are essential for staying abreast of evolving customer service trends and best practices. The customer service landscape is constantly evolving, driven by technological advancements, changing consumer behaviors, and emerging market trends. Service representatives must commit to lifelong learning, seeking out opportunities to enhance their skills, expand their knowledge, and stay updated on industry developments. This may involve participating in training programs, attending workshops and seminars, or pursuing professional certifications in customer service excellence.

Furthermore, a customer-centric mindset is fundamental to delivering exceptional service experiences. Service representatives must prioritize the needs, preferences, and satisfaction of customers above all else. This entails adopting a proactive approach to anticipating and addressing customer needs, going above and beyond expectations to deliver memorable service encounters. By aligning their actions and decisions with the overarching goal of customer satisfaction, representatives can cultivate a culture of service excellence that permeates throughout the organization.

In summary, customer service skills are indispensable in today's business landscape, driving customer satisfaction, loyalty, and advocacy. Effective communication, empathy, problem-solving, adaptability, professionalism, patience, resilience, continuous learning, and a customer-centric mindset are all essential components of exceptional customer service. By investing in the development and cultivation of these skills, businesses can elevate the quality of their service experiences, differentiate themselves from competitors, and foster lasting relationships with customers.

Chapter 2: Understanding Common Hardware Issues

Troubleshooting hardware failures is an essential skill for IT professionals tasked with maintaining the reliability and performance of computer systems. Hardware failures can manifest in various forms, ranging from simple malfunctions such as a non-responsive keyboard to more complex issues like system crashes or component failures. Effectively diagnosing and resolving hardware failures requires a systematic approach, encompassing diagnostic tools, troubleshooting techniques, and practical knowledge of hardware components.

One of the first steps in troubleshooting hardware failures is to identify the symptoms exhibited by the malfunctioning hardware. This may involve observing error messages, abnormal system behavior, or hardware indicators such as blinking lights or unusual noises. By gathering information about the symptoms, technicians can narrow down the scope of the problem and formulate an appropriate troubleshooting strategy.

Once the symptoms are identified, technicians can begin the diagnostic process by checking the physical connections and external peripherals associated with the malfunctioning hardware. For example, if a user reports that their monitor is not displaying any images, technicians may start by ensuring that the monitor's power cable is securely plugged in, and the video cable is properly connected to both the monitor and the computer's graphics card.

If the external connections appear to be intact, technicians may proceed to perform basic hardware tests to assess the functionality of individual components. Diagnostic tools such as built-in hardware diagnostics or third-party software utilities can be used to run tests on components such as the CPU, RAM, hard drive, and graphics card. For example, in a Windows environment, technicians can use the built-in Windows Memory Diagnostic tool (mdsched.exe) to check for memory errors, or third-party software such as Memtest86 for more comprehensive memory testing.

In addition to software-based diagnostic tools, technicians may also utilize hardware diagnostic devices such as multimeters or loopback plugs to test the electrical conductivity and functionality of hardware components. For example, technicians can use a multimeter to measure the voltage output of a power supply unit (PSU) or the resistance of a circuit on a motherboard to identify potential faults.

Furthermore, if the hardware failure is suspected to be caused by overheating or inadequate cooling, technicians may inspect the system's thermal management components, such as fans, heat sinks, and thermal paste. Accumulated dust and debris can obstruct airflow and cause components to overheat, leading to performance degradation or hardware failures. Technicians can use compressed air or antistatic brushes to clean out dust from cooling vents and components, ensuring optimal airflow and heat dissipation.

In cases where the hardware failure is attributed to a specific component, such as a faulty RAM module or a malfunctioning hard drive, technicians may need to replace the defective part to restore system functionality. For example, if a diagnostic test indicates that a RAM module is faulty, technicians can remove the defective module and install a replacement module of compatible specifications. Similarly, if a hard drive is failing due to bad sectors or mechanical issues, technicians can replace the failing drive with a new one and restore data from backups if necessary.

Moreover, software-related issues can sometimes masquerade as hardware failures, leading to misdiagnosis and unnecessary hardware replacements. Therefore, technicians should also consider software troubleshooting techniques such as updating device drivers, reinstalling operating system components, or performing system restores to resolve software-related conflicts or corruptions that may be causing hardware symptoms.

Additionally, documenting the troubleshooting process is essential for tracking progress, identifying recurring issues, and sharing knowledge with colleagues. Technicians should maintain detailed records of hardware failures, diagnostic tests performed, solutions implemented, and outcomes observed. This documentation can serve as a valuable reference for future troubleshooting efforts and contribute to the development of best practices and standardized procedures within the organization.

Furthermore, preventive maintenance measures can help mitigate the risk of hardware failures and prolong the lifespan of computer systems. Regularly scheduled maintenance tasks such as cleaning dust and debris, updating firmware and device drivers, and monitoring system temperatures can help identify potential issues before they escalate into full-fledged failures. By proactively addressing potential hardware issues, organizations can minimize downtime, reduce repair costs, and optimize the reliability and performance of their IT infrastructure.

In summary, troubleshooting hardware failures requires a systematic approach, encompassing diagnostic tools, practical knowledge of hardware components, and effective problem-solving skills. By accurately identifying symptoms, performing diagnostic tests, and implementing appropriate solutions, technicians can diagnose and resolve hardware failures efficiently, minimizing downtime and ensuring the reliability and performance of computer systems. Moreover, preventive maintenance measures and documentation practices are essential for mitigating the risk of future hardware failures and optimizing the long-term health of IT infrastructure.

Diagnosing peripheral device problems is a critical aspect of troubleshooting for IT professionals and individuals alike. Peripheral devices such as keyboards, mice, printers, and external storage devices play integral roles in computer systems, enhancing functionality and productivity. However, when these devices encounter issues, it can disrupt workflow and impede productivity. Effectively diagnosing peripheral device problems requires a systematic approach, encompassing both hardware and software troubleshooting techniques.

One of the first steps in diagnosing peripheral device problems is to check the physical connections and ensure that the device is properly connected to the computer. For wired peripherals such as keyboards, mice, and printers, technicians should inspect the cables for any signs of damage or wear and ensure that they are securely plugged into the appropriate ports on the computer. Similarly, for wireless peripherals, technicians should verify that the devices are powered on, and the wireless receivers are properly connected to the computer's USB ports.

If the physical connections appear to be intact, technicians can proceed to check the device settings and configurations in the operating system. In a Windows environment, technicians can use the Device Manager utility to view the status of peripheral devices, check for driver issues, and update device drivers if necessary. To access Device Manager, technicians can press the Windows key + X on the keyboard and select "Device Manager" from the menu, or they can run the command "devmgmt.msc" in the Run dialog box.

Similarly, in a macOS environment, technicians can use the System Information utility to view detailed information about connected peripherals and check for any driver or configuration issues. To access System Information, technicians can navigate to the "Apple" menu, select "About This Mac," and then click on the "System Report" button. From the System Report window, technicians can navigate to the "Hardware" section and select "USB" or "Bluetooth" to view information about connected peripherals.

In addition to checking device settings and configurations, technicians can also use diagnostic tools and utilities to test the functionality of peripheral devices. For example, keyboard testing software such as KeyboardTester.com or PassMark KeyboardTest can be used to check for keypress responsiveness, detect stuck or malfunctioning keys, and identify hardware issues with the keyboard. Similarly, mouse testing software such as MouseTester.com or

PassMark MouseTest can be used to evaluate mouse movement, button clicks, and scroll wheel functionality.

Furthermore, technicians can use built-in diagnostic tools and utilities provided by peripheral device manufacturers to troubleshoot specific issues. For example, printer manufacturers often provide diagnostic utilities that can help identify and resolve printing problems, such as print quality issues, paper jams, or connectivity issues. These utilities may include tools for cleaning print heads, aligning cartridges, or troubleshooting communication errors between the printer and the computer.

Moreover, if peripheral device problems persist despite troubleshooting efforts, technicians may need to perform more advanced troubleshooting steps, such as testing the device on another computer or reinstalling device drivers. Testing the device on another computer can help determine whether the issue is specific to the device itself or related to the computer's hardware or software configuration. If the device functions normally on another computer, the issue may be related to the original computer's configuration or drivers.

Additionally, reinstalling device drivers can help resolve driver-related issues that may be causing peripheral device problems. To reinstall device drivers in a Windows environment, technicians can use the Device Manager utility to uninstall the device driver, then restart the computer to allow Windows to automatically reinstall the driver. Alternatively, technicians can download the latest driver from the manufacturer's website and manually install it on the computer.

Furthermore, if peripheral device problems persist despite troubleshooting efforts, technicians may need to consider hardware repair or replacement options. For example, if a keyboard or mouse has physical damage or malfunctioning components that cannot be repaired, technicians may recommend replacing the device with a new one. Similarly, if a printer or external storage device experiences hardware failures such as mechanical issues or electronic component failures, technicians may advise replacing the device or seeking professional repair services.

In summary, diagnosing peripheral device problems requires a systematic approach, encompassing both hardware and software troubleshooting techniques. By checking physical connections, verifying device settings and configurations, using diagnostic tools and utilities, testing devices on other computers, reinstalling device drivers, and considering hardware repair or replacement options, technicians can effectively identify and resolve peripheral device problems, ensuring the reliability and functionality of computer systems. Moreover, proactive maintenance practices such as regular cleaning, updating drivers, and monitoring device performance can help prevent peripheral device problems and optimize the longevity of peripheral devices.

Chapter 3: Exploring Operating System Basics

Operating systems (OS) are the backbone of modern computing, serving as the interface between hardware components and user applications. They provide essential functionality such as managing hardware resources, facilitating communication between software and hardware, and providing a platform for running applications. However, the landscape of operating systems is diverse, with various options catering to different needs, preferences, and use cases.

One of the most widely used operating systems is Microsoft Windows, known for its user-friendly interface, broad compatibility with hardware and software, and extensive support for productivity applications. Windows operating systems such as Windows 10 and Windows 11 dominate the desktop computing market, offering features such as a graphical user interface (GUI), built-in security features, and support for multitasking and multimedia applications. Moreover, Windows operating systems are widely used in enterprise environments, providing robust management tools, network integration capabilities, and compatibility with business applications.

Another prominent operating system is macOS, developed by Apple Inc. and designed exclusively for Macintosh computers. macOS is known for its sleek and intuitive interface, seamless integration with Apple hardware and software, and strong emphasis on user experience and productivity. macOS offers features such as the Finder file manager, Spotlight search functionality, and the macOS App Store, providing users with access to a wide range of productivity, creativity, and entertainment applications. Additionally, macOS includes built-in security features such as Gatekeeper and FileVault, protecting users' data and privacy.

Linux is an open-source operating system renowned for its flexibility, stability, and customizability. Linux distributions such as Ubuntu, Fedora, and Debian cater to a diverse range of users, from casual desktop users to enterprise servers and embedded systems. Linux offers a command-line interface (CLI) as well as graphical user interfaces (GUIs) such as GNOME and KDE, providing users with a choice of interfaces and workflows. Moreover, Linux distributions are known for their robust security features, with built-in firewall tools, package management systems, and access control mechanisms.

In addition to mainstream operating systems, there are specialized operating systems designed for specific purposes and use cases. For example, Chrome OS is a lightweight operating system developed by Google and designed for Chromebook laptops and Chromebox desktops. Chrome OS is optimized for web-based applications and cloud computing, with a minimalistic interface, fast boot times, and seamless integration with Google services such as Gmail, Google Drive, and Google Classroom. Chrome OS also includes built-in security features such as automatic updates, sandboxed applications, and verified boot process.

Furthermore, mobile operating systems such as Android and iOS dominate the smartphone and tablet markets, providing users with a rich ecosystem of apps, games, and services. Android, developed by Google, is an open-source operating system based on the Linux kernel and designed for a wide range of devices, including smartphones, tablets, smartwatches, and smart TVs. Android offers features such as the Google Play Store, Google Assistant, and seamless integration with Google services such as Gmail, Google Maps, and Google Photos. Similarly, iOS, developed by Apple Inc., powers devices such as the iPhone, iPad, and iPod Touch, offering features such as the App Store, Siri voice assistant, and iCloud storage service.

Moreover, real-time operating systems (RTOS) are designed for embedded systems and time-critical applications such as industrial automation, automotive systems, and medical devices. RTOS such as FreeRTOS, VxWorks, and QNX provide deterministic behavior, low-latency response times, and support for multitasking and real-time scheduling. These operating systems are optimized for resource-constrained environments, with minimal overhead and efficient use of system resources. Additionally, server operating systems such as Windows Server, Linux server distributions, and FreeBSD are tailored for hosting and managing network services, websites, and applications. Server operating systems provide features such as server roles, virtualization support, and remote administration tools, enabling organizations to deploy and manage scalable and reliable server infrastructures. Moreover, server operating systems offer security features such as role-based access control (RBAC), encryption, and auditing capabilities to protect sensitive data and resources.

In summary, the landscape of operating systems is diverse, with various options catering to different needs, preferences, and use cases. Whether it's the user-friendly interface of Microsoft Windows, the sleek design of macOS, the flexibility of Linux, the simplicity of Chrome OS, the mobility of Android and iOS, the real-time capabilities of RTOS, or the scalability of server operating systems, each operating system offers unique features and advantages. By understanding the characteristics and capabilities of different operating systems, users can make informed decisions and choose the platform that best suits their requirements and objectives

Understanding the file system structure and navigation is fundamental to effectively managing files and directories within an operating system. The file system serves as the framework for organizing and storing data on storage devices such as hard drives, solid-state drives (SSDs), and network-attached storage (NAS) devices. By familiarizing oneself with the hierarchical structure of the file system and mastering navigation techniques, users can efficiently locate, create, modify, and delete files and directories to streamline their workflow and optimize storage utilization.

At the core of most operating systems lies the concept of a hierarchical file system, wherein files and directories are organized in a tree-like structure consisting of parent and child nodes. The root directory serves as the top-level directory in the hierarchy, from which all other directories and files are accessible. In Unix-like operating systems such as Linux and macOS, the root directory is denoted by a forward slash (/), while in Windows operating systems, it is represented by a backslash ().

To navigate the file system and view its structure, users can employ command-line interface (CLI) commands such as "ls" in Unix-like systems or "dir" in Windows. For instance, in Linux, typing "ls" and pressing Enter displays a list of files and directories in the current directory, while appending the "-l" option provides additional details such as file permissions, ownership, size, and modification date. Similarly, in Windows, typing "dir" and pressing Enter achieves a similar result, displaying a list of files and directories in the current directory.

Furthermore, users can navigate the file system by specifying relative or absolute paths to directories and files. A relative path refers to the location of a file or directory relative to the current working directory, while an absolute path specifies the complete path from the root directory. For example, in Unix-like systems, the path "./Documents" refers to the "Documents" directory within the current working directory, while the path "/home/user/Documents" specifies the "Documents" directory located at the specified absolute path. Likewise, in Windows, the path ".\Documents" and "C:\Users\User\Documents" represent relative and absolute paths, respectively.

Moreover, users can traverse directories and access files using navigation commands such as "cd" (change directory) in Unix-like systems or "cd" and "chdir" in Windows. For instance, typing "cd Documents" and pressing Enter changes the current working directory to the "Documents" directory in Unix-like systems, while in Windows, the command "cd Documents" or "chdir Documents" achieves the same result. Additionally, users can use the ".." notation to navigate to the parent directory or specify a relative path to navigate to a specific directory.

In addition to navigating directories and viewing file listings, users can create, copy, move, rename, and delete files and directories using CLI commands. For example, the "mkdir" command in Unix-like systems or "mkdir" in Windows allows users to create new directories, while the "touch" command in Unix-like systems or "echo" command in Windows can be used to create new files. Similarly, the "cp" (copy), "mv" (move), "rename" (rename), and "rm" (remove) commands enable users to copy, move, rename, and delete files and directories, respectively.

Furthermore, users can manipulate file permissions and ownership using CLI commands such as "chmod" and "chown" in Unix-like systems or "icacls" in Windows. For example, the "chmod" command allows users to modify file permissions, granting or revoking read, write, and execute permissions for the owner, group, and others. Similarly, the "chown" command enables users to change the ownership of files and directories, assigning ownership to specific users or groups.

Additionally, users can search for files and directories within the file system using CLI commands such as "find" in Unix-like systems or "dir" and "where" in Windows. For instance, the "find" command in Unix-like systems allows users to search for files based on various criteria such as file name, size, modification date, and permissions. In Windows, the "dir" command with the "/s" option recursively searches for files matching the specified criteria, while the "where" command searches for executable files matching the specified pattern within the system's path.

Moreover, users can perform disk space analysis and management using CLI commands such as "df" (disk free) and "du" (disk usage) in Unix-like systems or "dir" and "fsutil" in Windows. For example, the "df" command displays information about disk space usage, including total disk space, used space, and available space for mounted file systems. Similarly, the "du" command provides a summary of disk usage for files and directories within the specified directory.

In summary, understanding the file system structure and navigation is essential for effectively managing files and directories within an operating system. By mastering navigation techniques, CLI commands, and file manipulation operations, users can navigate the file system, create, modify, and delete files and directories, manipulate file permissions and ownership, search for files, and perform disk space analysis and management. These skills are invaluable for optimizing storage utilization, streamlining workflow, and maintaining an organized and efficient file system.

Chapter 4: Software Installation and Configuration

Installing and updating software is a fundamental aspect of managing computer systems, allowing users to access and utilize a wide range of applications and tools to meet their needs and objectives. Whether it's installing a new application to enhance productivity or updating existing software to patch security vulnerabilities and add new features, understanding the process of software installation and updating is essential for maintaining a secure, efficient, and up-to-date computing environment.

The process of installing software typically begins with obtaining the installation files from a trusted source, such as the official website of the software vendor or a reputable software distribution platform. Once the installation files are downloaded or obtained, users can proceed to initiate the installation process using the appropriate method for their operating system. In Unix-like systems such as Linux, software packages are typically distributed in package manager repositories, and users can install software using package manager commands such as "apt" in Debian-based systems or "yum" in Red Hat-based systems.

For example, to install a software package named "example" using the "apt" package manager in Debian-based systems, users can open a terminal window and type the command "sudo apt install example" followed by the Enter key. This command prompts the package manager to download and install the specified software package along with any dependencies required for its operation. Similarly, in Red Hat-based systems, users can use the "yum" package manager to install software packages by typing the command "sudo yum install example" in the terminal.

Moreover, package managers in Unix-like systems provide features for searching, updating, and removing software packages, allowing users to manage installed software efficiently. For instance, users can use the "apt search" command in Debian-based systems or the "yum search" command in Red Hat-based systems to search for available software packages matching a specific keyword. Additionally, the "apt update" and "yum update" commands can be used to update the package lists and install available updates for installed software packages.

In Windows operating systems, software installation typically involves running an executable installer file obtained from the software vendor's website or a trusted source. Once the installer file is downloaded or obtained, users can double-click on the file to initiate the installation process. This launches the software installer wizard, which guides users through the installation steps, such as selecting the installation directory, accepting license agreements, and configuring optional settings.

For example, to install a software application named "example" in Windows, users can navigate to the directory containing the downloaded installer file and double-click on the file to run it. This launches the installation wizard, which prompts users to follow on-screen instructions to complete the installation process. Once the installation is complete, users can launch the newly installed application from the Start menu or desktop shortcut.

Furthermore, users can update installed software in Windows by using built-in update mechanisms provided by software vendors or utilizing third-party software update management tools. Many software applications include automatic update features that periodically check for available updates and prompt users to install them. Alternatively, users can manually check for updates by opening the application's settings or preferences menu and navigating to the "Updates" or "Check for Updates" section.

Additionally, users can utilize third-party software update management tools such as Ninite, Patch My PC, or Chocolatey to automate the process of updating installed software across multiple applications. These tools offer centralized management features, allowing users to view available updates for installed software, select specific updates to install, and schedule automated update tasks. Moreover, some tools provide additional features such as patch management, software inventory, and reporting capabilities to streamline software update management processes.

In Unix-like systems, software updates are typically managed using package managers, which provide features for installing updates for installed software packages. Users can use the "apt upgrade" command in Debian-based systems or the "yum update" command in Red Hat-based systems to install available updates for installed software packages. These commands download and install the latest versions of software packages along with any dependencies required for the update.

Furthermore, users can automate software updates in Unix-like systems by configuring package manager repositories to automatically check for updates and install them on a scheduled basis. This can be achieved by configuring the package manager's update settings or using third-party tools such as cron jobs or systemd timers to schedule update tasks. By automating software updates, users can ensure that their systems remain up-to-date with the latest security patches and feature enhancements without manual intervention.

Moreover, users can manage software installations and updates in mobile operating systems such as Android and iOS using app stores provided by platform vendors. App stores such as the Google Play Store for Android and the App Store for iOS offer a curated selection of applications, allowing users to browse, install, and update software directly from their mobile devices. Users can navigate to the app store, search for the desired application, and tap the "Install" or "Update" button to initiate the installation or update process.

In summary, installing and updating software is essential for maintaining a secure, efficient, and up-to-date computing environment. By following the appropriate installation procedures for their operating system, users can install new software applications to meet their needs and objectives. Additionally, by staying vigilant and applying available updates for installed software, users can ensure that their systems remain protected against security vulnerabilities and benefit from the latest features and enhancements offered by software vendors.

Configuring software settings and preferences is an essential aspect of personalizing and optimizing the user experience within various applications and tools. Whether it's customizing the appearance, adjusting functionality, or fine-tuning performance, understanding how to configure software settings allows users to tailor their computing environment to suit their individual needs and preferences. From productivity software and web browsers to operating system settings and multimedia applications, mastering the art of software configuration empowers users to maximize efficiency, streamline workflows, and enhance usability across their digital ecosystem.

At the heart of software configuration lies the ability to access and manipulate settings and preferences through intuitive user interfaces or command-line interfaces (CLI). Graphical user interfaces (GUIs) provide users with visual controls, menus, and options for adjusting settings and preferences, while CLI commands offer a more direct and efficient method for experienced users to modify configurations. By leveraging these interfaces, users can navigate through various configuration menus, dialogs, and panels to customize software behavior according to their preferences.

In GUI-based applications, accessing settings and preferences typically involves navigating through menus and submenus to locate the desired configuration options. For example, in productivity software such as Microsoft Word or Google Docs, users can access settings related to formatting, spell check, auto-correction, and language preferences by clicking on the "File" menu, selecting "Options" or "Preferences," and then exploring the available tabs and sections. Within these menus, users can toggle switches, adjust sliders, and enter values to customize the behavior of the application to their liking.

Similarly, in web browsers such as Google Chrome, Mozilla Firefox, or Microsoft Edge, users can access settings and preferences by clicking on the menu icon (often represented by three horizontal lines or dots) and selecting "Settings" or "Preferences" from the dropdown menu. Within the settings menu, users can configure various options related to browsing behavior, privacy and security settings, appearance and theme preferences, and advanced settings such as proxy configurations and experimental features. Additionally, users can install browser extensions or add-ons to further extend the functionality and customization options available within their web browser.

Moreover, operating systems such as Windows, macOS, and Linux offer extensive settings menus and control panels for configuring system-wide settings and preferences. In Windows, users can access the Control Panel or Settings app to adjust settings related to system and security, devices, network and internet, personalization, and more. Similarly, in macOS, users can access System Preferences to configure settings related to appearance, notifications, security and privacy, energy saver, and accessibility. In Linux distributions, users can customize system settings using desktop environments such as GNOME, KDE, or Xfce, which provide centralized settings panels for adjusting various system configurations.

In addition to GUI-based configuration interfaces, CLI commands provide a powerful and efficient means for configuring software settings and preferences, particularly for advanced users and system administrators. CLI commands allow users to modify configuration files, run scripts, and execute commands to automate repetitive tasks and configure settings at scale. For example, in Unix-like systems such as Linux, users can edit text-based configuration files using command-line text editors such as Vim or Nano, or manipulate configuration settings using command-line utilities such as "sed" (stream editor) or "awk" (pattern scanning and processing language).

Furthermore, many software applications and operating systems support configuration management tools and scripting languages that enable users to automate software configuration tasks and enforce consistent configurations across multiple systems. Tools such as Ansible, Puppet, Chef, and PowerShell Desired State Configuration (DSC) provide infrastructure-as-code capabilities, allowing users to define configuration settings in declarative code and apply them to target systems automatically. By using configuration management tools, users can ensure that software settings and preferences are standardized, auditable, and easily reproducible across diverse computing environments.

Moreover, cloud-based services and applications often offer web-based dashboards or APIs for configuring settings and preferences remotely. For example, cloud computing platforms such as Amazon Web Services (AWS), Microsoft Azure, and Google Cloud Platform (GCP) provide web-based consoles and command-line interfaces for managing cloud resources, configuring security settings, and optimizing performance. Similarly, Software-as-a-Service (SaaS) applications such as Salesforce, Microsoft 365, and Slack offer web-based administration portals for configuring user settings, access controls, and integration options.

Additionally, mobile operating systems such as Android and iOS provide settings apps or menus for configuring device settings, network preferences, app permissions, and system preferences. Users can access these settings menus by navigating to the device's settings app or swiping down from the top of the screen to access quick settings toggles and shortcuts. Within the settings menu, users can adjust options such as display brightness, sound volume, Wi-Fi and Bluetooth settings, app notifications, and battery optimization settings to customize their mobile experience.

In summary, configuring software settings and preferences is a fundamental aspect of personalizing and optimizing the user experience across various applications, tools, and operating systems. Whether through GUI-based interfaces, CLI commands, configuration management tools, or cloud-based consoles, users have access to a wide range of options for customizing software behavior to suit their individual needs and preferences. By mastering the art of software configuration, users can streamline workflows, enhance usability, and maximize efficiency within their digital ecosystem.

Chapter 5: Introduction to Networking Concepts

Networking protocols are the foundation of modern communication networks, facilitating the exchange of data and information between devices and systems across local and global networks. From the physical layer to the application layer, networking protocols define the rules, conventions, and standards that govern how data is transmitted, routed, and processed within networked environments. Understanding the various networking protocols is essential for network administrators, IT professionals, and individuals alike, as it enables them to design, deploy, and manage networks effectively while ensuring interoperability, security, and reliability.

At the physical layer of the networking stack, protocols such as Ethernet, Wi-Fi, and Bluetooth define the mechanisms for transmitting data over physical media such as copper cables, fiber-optic cables, and wireless radio waves. Ethernet, the most widely used wired networking protocol, specifies standards for data framing, collision detection, and media access control (MAC) addressing. Devices connected to an Ethernet network communicate using Ethernet frames, which contain source and destination MAC addresses, data payload, and error-checking information. CLI command: "ipconfig /all" or "ifconfig -a" to view network interface configuration.

In contrast, Wi-Fi (IEEE 802.11) and Bluetooth (IEEE 802.15.1) are wireless networking protocols that enable communication between devices over radio frequencies. Wi-Fi protocols define standards for wireless local area networks (WLANs), including data modulation, channel allocation, and security mechanisms such as Wi-Fi Protected Access (WPA) and WPA2. Bluetooth protocols, on the other hand, facilitate short-range communication between devices such as smartphones, tablets, and wearable devices, allowing for wireless data transfer, audio streaming, and device pairing.

Moving up the networking stack to the data link layer, protocols such as Address Resolution Protocol (ARP) and Point-to-Point Protocol (PPP) govern communication between devices within the same network or across wide area networks (WANs). ARP is responsible for mapping IP addresses to MAC addresses within a local network, allowing devices to communicate with each other based on their hardware addresses. When a device needs to communicate with another device on the same network, it sends an ARP request to resolve the MAC address associated with the target IP address. CLI command: "arp - a" to view ARP cache table.

PPP, on the other hand, is a protocol used for establishing and maintaining point-to-point connections between two devices over serial links such as dial-up connections or leased lines. PPP defines standards for encapsulating and transmitting data packets over serial links, including authentication mechanisms, error detection, and packet framing. In addition to PPP, High-Level Data Link Control (HDLC) is another data link layer protocol commonly used for synchronous serial communication between devices. CLI command: "ppp" or "hdlc" to configure PPP or HDLC settings.

At the network layer, protocols such as Internet Protocol (IP), Internet Control Message Protocol (ICMP), and Routing Information Protocol (RIP) play key roles in routing and forwarding data packets between networks. IP is a fundamental protocol that provides addressing and routing functions, enabling devices to communicate with each other across interconnected networks. IP addresses uniquely identify devices on a network and determine how data packets are routed from a source to a destination. CLI command: "ip address show" to view IP address configuration.

ICMP is a supporting protocol used for diagnostic and error reporting purposes within IP networks. ICMP messages such as ping and traceroute are commonly used to test network connectivity, measure round-trip times, and identify network issues. Ping sends ICMP echo request messages to a target device and waits for an echo reply, while traceroute traces the path that packets take from the source to the destination, showing each hop along the way. CLI command: "ping" or "traceroute" to test network connectivity.

RIP is a distance-vector routing protocol used for exchanging routing information between devices within an autonomous system. RIP routers broadcast routing updates containing information about reachable networks and their associated metrics, allowing routers to dynamically update their routing tables and determine the best path to reach a destination. However, RIP has limitations such as slow convergence and limited scalability, making it less suitable for large and complex networks. CLI command: "show ip route" to view routing table entries.

Moving up to the transport layer, protocols such as Transmission Control Protocol (TCP) and User Datagram Protocol (UDP) provide reliable and connectionless communication services, respectively. TCP is a connection-oriented protocol that ensures the reliable delivery of data packets by establishing a virtual circuit between the sender and receiver, acknowledging received packets, and retransmitting lost or corrupted packets. TCP also implements flow control and congestion control mechanisms to manage data transmission rates and prevent network congestion. CLI command: "netstat -t" to view TCP connections.

In contrast, UDP is a connectionless protocol that provides best-effort delivery of data packets without the overhead of establishing a connection or maintaining state information. UDP is commonly used for time-sensitive applications such as real-time streaming, voice over IP (VoIP), and online gaming, where occasional packet loss or out-of-order delivery is acceptable. However, UDP does not provide reliability, flow control, or congestion control mechanisms, leaving these responsibilities to higher-layer protocols or applications. CLI command: "netstat -u" to view UDP connections.

At the application layer, protocols such as Hypertext Transfer Protocol (HTTP), File Transfer Protocol (FTP), and Simple Mail Transfer Protocol (SMTP) enable communication between applications and services running on different devices. HTTP is the foundation of the World Wide Web, facilitating the transfer of hypertext documents (web pages) between web servers and web clients (browsers). HTTP defines standards for requesting and delivering web resources, including methods such as GET, POST, PUT, and DELETE. CLI command: "curl" or "wget" to perform HTTP requests.

FTP is a protocol used for transferring files between a client and a server over a network connection. FTP clients connect to FTP servers and authenticate using a username and password, allowing users to upload, download, and manage files and directories on remote servers. FTP supports two modes of data transfer: active mode, where the server initiates the data connection, and passive mode, where the client initiates the data connection. CLI command: "ftp" to connect to an FTP server and transfer files.

SMTP is a protocol used for sending email messages between mail servers over the internet. SMTP clients (mail user agents) submit outgoing email messages to SMTP servers (mail transfer agents) for delivery to the recipient's mailbox. SMTP defines standards for message format, message encoding, and message delivery, including commands such as HELO, MAIL FROM, RCPT TO, DATA, and QUIT. CLI command: "telnet" to connect to an SMTP server and manually send email messages.

In summary, networking protocols form the backbone of communication networks, defining the rules, conventions, and standards for transmitting and processing data between devices and systems. From the physical layer to the application layer, each protocol serves a specific purpose and plays a critical role in enabling networked communication, routing, and application services. By understanding the characteristics and functionalities of different networking protocols, network administrators, IT professionals, and individuals can design, deploy, and manage networks effectively while ensuring interoperability, security, and reliability.

Local Area Networks (LANs) and Wide Area Networks (WANs) are two fundamental types of computer networks that play distinct roles in facilitating communication and data exchange between devices and systems. LANs are typically confined to a specific geographic area, such as a home, office building, or campus, and connect devices within close proximity to each other. In contrast, WANs span larger geographical areas and interconnect multiple LANs, enabling communication between devices across vast distances. By understanding the characteristics, components, and functionalities of LANs and WANs, network administrators, IT professionals, and individuals can design, deploy, and manage networks effectively to meet their organization's connectivity requirements.

At the heart of every LAN is a network infrastructure consisting of interconnected devices such as computers, servers, printers, routers, switches, and access points. These devices are connected using various networking technologies such as Ethernet, Wi-Fi, and Bluetooth, allowing for the transmission of data packets between devices within the same physical location. Ethernet, the most widely used wired networking technology, employs twisted-pair copper cables or fiber-optic cables to establish wired connections between devices, while Wi-Fi and Bluetooth provide wireless connectivity options for mobile and portable devices. CLI command: "ipconfig /all" to view network interface configuration.

LANs are characterized by high data transfer rates, low latency, and minimal network congestion, making them ideal for local communication and resource sharing within organizations. LANs often utilize Ethernet switches to facilitate communication between devices by forwarding data packets based on MAC addresses. Switches operate at the data link layer of the networking stack and use MAC address tables to determine the appropriate port for forwarding incoming data packets to their destination devices. CLI command: "show mac address-table" to view MAC address table entries.

In addition to switches, LANs may also incorporate routers to facilitate communication between multiple LANs or to provide connectivity to external networks such as the internet. Routers operate at the network layer of the networking stack and use IP addresses to route data packets between different networks. By examining the destination IP address of incoming data packets, routers determine the optimal path for forwarding packets to their destination networks. CLI command: "show ip route" to view routing table entries.

LANs may also include network servers that provide centralized services such as file storage, printing, authentication, and application hosting to networked devices. File servers allow users to store and share files across the network, while print servers enable users to send print jobs to network-connected printers. Authentication servers, such as domain controllers in Windows environments, authenticate user credentials and enforce access control policies for network resources. Application servers host and deliver software applications or services to networked clients, such as web servers hosting websites or database servers storing and retrieving data. CLI command: "net share" to view shared resources on a Windows file server.

Wide Area Networks (WANs), on the other hand, extend beyond the boundaries of a single location and interconnect multiple LANs dispersed across different geographical areas. WANs utilize networking technologies such as leased lines, circuit-switched networks, packet-switched networks, and virtual private networks (VPNs) to establish connectivity between geographically distant locations. Leased lines, such as T1/E1 lines, provide dedicated point-to-point connections between two locations, offering guaranteed bandwidth and reliability but at a higher cost. CLI command: "show interface serial" to view serial interface configuration.

Circuit-switched networks, such as the Public Switched Telephone Network (PSTN), establish temporary connections between devices using circuit-switching techniques, where a dedicated communication channel is reserved for the duration of a call. Packet-switched networks, such as the internet, transmit data packets between devices using packet-switching techniques, where data packets are routed dynamically based on destination IP addresses. VPNs leverage encryption and tunneling protocols to create secure and private communication channels over public networks, enabling remote users to access corporate resources securely. CLI command: "show crypto ipsec sa" to view IPSec security associations.

WANs often rely on routers and wide area network switches (WAN switches) to facilitate communication between different LANs and to provide connectivity to external networks and internet services. WAN routers operate at the network layer and use routing protocols such as Border Gateway Protocol (BGP) and Open Shortest Path First (OSPF) to exchange routing information and determine optimal paths for forwarding data packets across the WAN. WAN switches, such as multiservice access platforms (MSAPs) or carrier Ethernet switches, enable service providers to aggregate and switch traffic between multiple customer LANs. CLI command: "show ip bgp neighbors" to view BGP neighbor relationships.

Moreover, WANs may utilize additional networking technologies such as Multiprotocol Label Switching (MPLS), Asynchronous Transfer Mode (ATM), and Frame Relay to optimize traffic routing, prioritize data packets, and ensure Quality of Service (QoS) for critical applications. MPLS allows service providers to establish virtual private networks (VPNs) and prioritize traffic based on predefined service classes, ensuring reliable and predictable performance for latency-sensitive applications such as voice and video. ATM and Frame Relay are legacy WAN technologies that provide virtual circuit-based connections and Quality of Service (QoS) features for traffic prioritization and congestion management. CLI command: "show mpls ldp neighbor" to view MPLS LDP neighbors.

In addition to physical WAN connections, organizations may deploy software-defined WAN (SD-WAN) solutions to optimize network performance, reduce costs, and simplify management across distributed locations. SD-WAN solutions utilize software-based controllers to dynamically route traffic over multiple WAN links such as broadband internet, MPLS, and LTE, based on predefined policies and network conditions. By intelligently load balancing and prioritizing traffic, SD-WAN solutions improve application performance, enhance security, and increase reliability for branch office connectivity. CLI command: "show sdwan status" to view SD-WAN status information.

In summary, understanding the characteristics, components, and functionalities of LANs and WANs is essential for designing, deploying, and managing network infrastructure effectively. While LANs provide localized connectivity and resource sharing within a single location, WANs extend connectivity across larger geographical areas and interconnect multiple LANs to facilitate communication between distributed locations. By leveraging appropriate networking technologies and protocols, organizations can establish reliable, secure, and scalable networks that meet their connectivity requirements and support business operations efficiently.

Chapter 6: Basic Troubleshooting Techniques

Identifying and isolating problems is a crucial aspect of troubleshooting in various technical domains, including IT, networking, electronics, and engineering. Whether it's diagnosing software glitches, pinpointing hardware failures, or resolving network connectivity issues, the ability to systematically identify and isolate problems is essential for maintaining operational efficiency, minimizing downtime, and ensuring the reliability of systems and services. By employing effective problem-solving techniques, diagnostic tools, and troubleshooting methodologies, technicians, engineers, and IT professionals can efficiently identify root causes, implement corrective actions, and restore functionality to malfunctioning systems and components.

One of the initial steps in identifying and isolating problems is gathering relevant information about the symptoms, behaviors, and environmental factors associated with the issue. This may involve interviewing users or stakeholders affected by the problem to understand their observations, documenting error messages or warning signs displayed by systems or devices, and reviewing system logs or diagnostic reports for any anomalies or irregularities. CLI command: "tail -f /var/log/syslog" to monitor system logs in real-time.

Once sufficient information has been collected, technicians can begin the process of systematically diagnosing the problem by performing diagnostic tests, troubleshooting procedures, and root cause analysis. In IT and software troubleshooting, techniques such as divide and conquer, binary search, and regression testing may be employed to isolate problematic software components, identify conflicting configurations, or validate software updates and patches. CLI command: "traceroute" to trace the route to a destination IP address.

Similarly, in networking troubleshooting, technicians may use network monitoring tools such as ping, traceroute, and network analyzers to diagnose connectivity issues, measure network performance, and identify bottlenecks or packet loss. Ping is a utility used to test the reachability of a host on an IP network by sending ICMP echo request packets and waiting for ICMP echo reply packets. Traceroute is a diagnostic tool used to trace the route that packets take from the source to the destination, showing each hop along the way. CLI command: "ping" to test network connectivity.

Furthermore, network analyzers such as Wireshark or tcpdump allow technicians to capture and analyze network traffic in real-time, enabling them to identify protocol errors, analyze packet contents, and detect network anomalies such as excessive broadcast traffic, network loops, or denial-of-service (DoS) attacks. By examining packet headers and payloads, technicians can gain insights into the behavior of networked devices, identify misconfigurations or security vulnerabilities, and troubleshoot network performance issues. CLI command: "tcpdump -i eth0" to capture network traffic on a specific interface.

In hardware troubleshooting, technicians may use diagnostic tools such as multimeters, oscilloscopes, and logic analyzers to test and analyze the electrical signals, voltages, and waveforms produced by electronic components and circuits. Multimeters are versatile tools used to measure voltage, current, resistance, and continuity in electronic circuits, allowing technicians to identify faulty components, open circuits, or short circuits. Oscilloscopes display graphical representations of electrical signals over time, enabling technicians to visualize waveforms, detect abnormalities, and diagnose signal integrity issues.

Moreover, logic analyzers are specialized tools used to capture, display, and analyze digital signals and waveforms in digital circuits and systems. Logic analyzers provide detailed insights into the behavior of digital signals, enabling technicians to debug digital logic circuits, troubleshoot communication protocols, and verify the operation of microcontrollers, FPGAs, and embedded systems. By examining signal timing, protocol sequences, and state transitions, technicians can identify timing violations, protocol errors, or logic faults affecting system operation.

In mechanical and engineering troubleshooting, technicians may employ visual inspection, measurement tools, and performance testing to identify and isolate problems in mechanical systems, machinery, and equipment. Visual inspection involves visually inspecting components, assemblies, and structures for signs of wear, damage, or misalignment, such as cracks, leaks, or corrosion. Measurement tools such as calipers, micrometers, and dial indicators allow technicians to accurately measure dimensions, tolerances, and clearances in mechanical components, aiding in the detection of dimensional deviations or assembly errors.

Furthermore, performance testing involves evaluating the performance characteristics, operating parameters, and functional capabilities of mechanical systems under normal or simulated operating conditions. Performance tests may include load testing, stress testing, endurance testing, and vibration analysis to assess the mechanical strength, durability, and reliability of components and assemblies. By subjecting mechanical systems to controlled tests and monitoring their responses, technicians can identify weaknesses, design flaws, or material defects that may lead to operational failures or malfunctions.

In summary, identifying and isolating problems is a critical skill in troubleshooting across various technical disciplines, including IT, networking, electronics, and engineering. By systematically gathering information, performing diagnostic tests, and analyzing system behavior, technicians can effectively identify root causes, isolate problematic components, and implement corrective actions to resolve issues and restore functionality to systems and services. Through continuous learning, experience, and collaboration, technicians can refine their problem-solving skills and become proficient troubleshooters in their respective fields.

Troubleshooting is an essential skill for anyone involved in managing computer systems, networks, and IT infrastructure. Whether you're a seasoned IT professional or a novice user, encountering technical issues and problems is inevitable in the world of technology. Step-by-step troubleshooting methodologies provide a structured approach for identifying, analyzing, and resolving problems efficiently, thereby minimizing downtime, optimizing system performance, and enhancing productivity. By following a systematic troubleshooting process, individuals can effectively diagnose and address a wide range of technical issues, from software glitches and hardware failures to network connectivity problems and system errors.

The first step in any troubleshooting methodology is to gather information and define the problem accurately. This involves identifying the symptoms of the issue, understanding its impact on system functionality, and gathering relevant details such as error messages, system logs, and user reports. By collecting comprehensive information about the problem, troubleshooters can gain insights into its root cause and develop an effective strategy for resolution. CLI command: "dmesg" to view kernel ring buffer messages.

Once the problem is defined, the next step is to isolate the root cause through systematic testing and analysis. This often involves dividing the problem space into smaller, manageable components and testing each component independently to identify the source of the issue. Troubleshooters can use diagnostic tools, monitoring utilities, and testing methodologies to isolate faulty components and narrow down potential causes. For example, if a computer is experiencing network connectivity issues, troubleshooters can use the "ping" command to test network connectivity to remote hosts and the "traceroute" command to trace the route packets take to reach their destination.

After isolating the root cause of the problem, troubleshooters can develop and implement a plan of action to resolve the issue effectively. This may involve applying known solutions or workarounds, performing software updates or patches, replacing faulty hardware components, or reconfiguring system settings. Troubleshooters should prioritize solutions based on their impact on system functionality, urgency, and feasibility, and communicate the plan of action to stakeholders as needed. CLI command: "yum update" to update packages on a CentOS/RHEL system.

Throughout the troubleshooting process, it's essential to document all steps taken, including diagnostic tests performed, solutions applied, and outcomes observed. This documentation serves as a record of the troubleshooting process, allowing troubleshooters to track their progress, share insights with colleagues, and refer back to previous cases for reference. Additionally, documentation provides valuable insights into recurring issues, patterns of failure, and areas for improvement, enabling organizations to develop preventive measures and enhance their overall IT infrastructure. CLI command: "journalctl" to view system journal logs.

In addition to technical skills and knowledge, effective troubleshooting requires critical thinking, problem-solving abilities, and the ability to work under pressure. Troubleshooters should be able to analyze complex problems, identify patterns and trends, and develop innovative solutions to address them. Moreover, troubleshooting often involves collaboration with colleagues, vendors, and support personnel, requiring effective communication skills and teamwork. By fostering a collaborative and supportive environment, organizations can leverage the collective expertise of their teams to tackle even the most challenging technical issues effectively.

Furthermore, continuous learning and professional development are essential for mastering troubleshooting methodologies and staying abreast of emerging technologies and best practices. Troubleshooters should regularly update their skills, pursue certifications, and participate in training programs to expand their knowledge and expertise in areas such as networking, cybersecurity, cloud computing, and software development. By investing in ongoing education and skills development, individuals can enhance their troubleshooting capabilities and become invaluable assets to their organizations.

In summary, step-by-step troubleshooting methodologies provide a structured approach for identifying, analyzing, and resolving technical issues efficiently. By following a systematic troubleshooting process, individuals can isolate the root cause of problems, develop effective solutions, and minimize downtime, thereby optimizing system performance and enhancing productivity. With the right combination of technical skills, critical thinking abilities, and collaboration, troubleshooters can tackle even the most challenging technical issues with confidence and competence.

Chapter 7: Resolving Printer Problems

Printer connectivity issues are a common source of frustration for users and IT support personnel alike, often leading to delays in printing tasks, reduced productivity, and increased workload for troubleshooting. Whether it's a network printer that refuses to print, a wireless printer that won't connect to the network, or a USB printer that isn't recognized by the computer, resolving printer connectivity issues requires a systematic approach, attention to detail, and familiarity with printer hardware, drivers, and network configurations. By following a structured troubleshooting process and leveraging diagnostic tools and techniques, individuals can identify and address printer connectivity issues effectively, restoring printing functionality and minimizing disruptions in workflow.

The first step in troubleshooting printer connectivity issues is to verify the physical connections and power supply. Ensure that the printer is powered on, properly connected to the electrical outlet, and that all cables, including USB, Ethernet, or power cables, are securely plugged in. Additionally, check for any error messages or indicator lights on the printer's control panel that may indicate hardware problems or connectivity issues. For network printers, verify that the Ethernet cable is connected to the correct port on the printer and the network switch or router. CLI command: "ipconfig" (Windows) or "ifconfig" (Linux/macOS) to check network interface configuration.

Next, check the status of the printer in the operating system's printer settings or control panel. Ensure that the printer is set as the default printer and that it is online and available for printing. In Windows, open the Control Panel, navigate to Devices and Printers, and check the status of the printer. If the printer is listed as offline or unavailable, right-click on the printer icon and select "Use Printer Online" to restore connectivity. In macOS, open System Preferences, select Printers & Scanners, and check the status of the printer. CLI command: "lpstat -p" to check printer status in Unix-like systems.

If the printer is connected to a network, troubleshoot network connectivity issues by checking the network settings and configuration. Verify that the printer is assigned a valid IP address, subnet mask, and default gateway, and that it is configured to use the correct network protocol (e.g., TCP/IP). Use network diagnostic tools such as ping, traceroute, or network scanning utilities to test connectivity to the printer from the computer or other devices on the network. If necessary, reset the printer's network settings and reconfigure the network connection. CLI command: "ping" or "traceroute" to test network connectivity.

Ensure that the printer drivers are installed correctly and up-to-date on the computer. Printer drivers act as a bridge between the operating system and the printer hardware, enabling communication and data transfer between the two. If the printer drivers are outdated or corrupted, it can lead to connectivity issues and printing errors. To update printer drivers in Windows, open

Device Manager, locate the printer under Printers, right-click on it, and select "Update Driver." In macOS, open System Preferences, select Printers & Scanners, and click on the "+" button to add a new printer or update existing drivers. CLI command: "apt-get" (Linux) or "brew" (macOS) to update printer drivers.

For wireless printers, troubleshoot wireless connectivity issues by checking the wireless network settings and signal strength. Ensure that the printer is connected to the correct wireless network and that the wireless signal is strong and stable. Move the printer closer to the wireless router or access point to improve signal strength, or consider adding a wireless range extender or repeater to extend coverage. If necessary, reset the printer's wireless settings and reconnect it to the wireless network. CLI command: "iwconfig" (Linux) or "airport" (macOS) to view wireless network information.

If the printer connectivity issues persist, perform a factory reset on the printer to restore it to its default settings. Keep in mind that performing a factory reset will erase all custom settings and configurations, so it should be done as a last resort. Consult the printer's user manual or manufacturer's website for instructions on how to perform a factory reset. After performing the factory reset, reconfigure the printer settings, network connections, and drivers as needed. CLI command: "reset" or "restore-defaults" (specific command varies by printer model).

In addition to troubleshooting printer connectivity issues locally, consider seeking assistance from the printer manufacturer's technical support or online forums and communities. Many printer manufacturers offer online support resources, troubleshooting guides, and driver downloads on their websites to help users resolve common printer problems. Alternatively, seek assistance from IT support personnel or consultants with experience in printer troubleshooting and network management. By leveraging external resources and expertise, individuals can expedite the resolution of printer connectivity issues and minimize downtime. CLI command: "man" (Linux) or "help" (Windows/macOS) to access printer documentation or support resources.

In summary, printer connectivity issues can be frustrating and disruptive, but they can be resolved effectively by following a structured troubleshooting process and leveraging diagnostic tools and techniques. By verifying physical connections, checking printer settings, drivers, and network configurations, and seeking assistance from manufacturer support or IT professionals, individuals can identify and address printer connectivity issues efficiently, restoring printing functionality and minimizing disruptions in workflow. With persistence, patience, and attention to detail, printer connectivity issues can be resolved, allowing users to resume printing tasks and maintain productivity.

Print job queuing and management are integral aspects of print infrastructure administration, crucial for ensuring efficient use of printing resources, optimizing print job flow, and maintaining productivity in organizations of all sizes. Whether it's a single office printer or a networked printing environment with multiple printers serving a large user base, effective print job queuing and management techniques help streamline printing operations, minimize print job conflicts, and prioritize printing tasks based on user needs and organizational requirements. By implementing robust print job queuing and management strategies, administrators can enhance print system performance, reduce printing costs, and improve overall user satisfaction.

One fundamental aspect of print job management is the establishment of print queues, which serve as virtual placeholders for print jobs awaiting processing and output. Print queues are created for each physical printer or printer pool within the print server environment, enabling users to submit print jobs to specific printers or queues for printing. Print queues can be configured with various settings and options, including printer properties, paper size, print quality, duplex printing, and job scheduling parameters, allowing administrators to tailor print job processing to meet specific requirements. CLI command: "lpadmin" (Linux/macOS) or "printui" (Windows) to create or configure print queues.

To manage print queues effectively, administrators can implement print job prioritization techniques to ensure that critical or time-sensitive print jobs are processed and printed promptly. Print job prioritization can be based on factors such as user privileges, job attributes, print server load, and printer availability. For example, administrators can assign higher priority levels to print jobs submitted by executives or management staff, ensuring that their documents are printed without delay. Similarly, print jobs with urgent or high-priority status can be processed ahead of standard print jobs in the queue. CLI command: "lpadmin -p PRINTER_NAME -o job-sheets=none, job-priority=1" to set print job priority.

In addition to prioritizing print jobs, administrators can implement print job scheduling techniques to manage print job flow and optimize printer usage. Print job scheduling involves configuring print queues to process print jobs at specific times or intervals, reducing print server congestion during peak usage periods and maximizing printer availability. For example, administrators can schedule large print jobs or print jobs with high resource requirements (e.g., color printing) to be processed during off-peak hours or overnight when printer usage is minimal. Similarly, administrators can stagger print job processing across multiple printers to distribute workload evenly and prevent bottlenecks. CLI command: "at" (Linux/macOS) or "schtasks" (Windows) to schedule print jobs.

To facilitate print job tracking and monitoring, administrators can implement print job logging and auditing mechanisms to capture detailed information about print job activity, including user identity, document name, print job attributes, and printing timestamps. Print job logs provide valuable insights into printing patterns, user behavior, and resource utilization, allowing administrators to identify potential issues, enforce printing policies, and allocate printing resources effectively. Moreover, print job logs can be used for auditing and compliance purposes, helping organizations ensure accountability and regulatory compliance. CLI command: "cupsctl LogLevel=debug" to enable verbose logging in CUPS (Common Unix Printing System).

Another aspect of print job management is print job routing, which involves directing print jobs to the most appropriate printer or print queue based on predefined criteria such as printer availability, location, or print job characteristics. Print job routing helps distribute printing workload evenly across multiple printers, balance print server load, and minimize print job delays and bottlenecks. For example, administrators can configure print servers to automatically route color print jobs to color printers and black-and-white print jobs to monochrome printers, optimizing printer usage and reducing printing costs. CLI command: "lpmove" (Linux/macOS) or "Print Management" (Windows) to configure print job routing rules.

To streamline print job submission and management for users, administrators can implement print job submission portals or web interfaces that allow users to submit print jobs remotely from their desktops, laptops, or mobile devices. Print job submission portals provide users with a centralized platform for submitting, managing, and tracking print jobs, enabling them to select printers, adjust print settings, and monitor print job status in real-time. Moreover, print job submission portals can support advanced features such as print job release, secure printing, and cost accounting, enhancing user convenience and print system security. CLI command: "cupsctl WebInterface=yes" to enable the CUPS web interface.

In addition to managing print jobs at the print server level, administrators can deploy print management software solutions that offer advanced print job queuing and management capabilities, such as centralized print queue management, print job routing, quota management, and reporting. Print management software solutions provide administrators with centralized control over printing resources, allowing them to enforce printing policies, monitor print job activity, and generate detailed reports and analytics. Moreover, print management software solutions integrate with directory services and authentication systems, enabling user authentication and access control for printing. CLI command: "lpd" (Linux/macOS) or "Print Management Console" (Windows) to configure print management software.

Furthermore, administrators can leverage printer pooling techniques to improve printer availability, redundancy, and fault tolerance in print server environments with multiple printers. Printer pooling involves grouping multiple printers of the same type or model into a single logical printer object, allowing print jobs to be distributed dynamically among the available printers in the pool. Printer pooling helps distribute printing workload evenly, reduce print job processing times, and ensure uninterrupted printing operations in the event of printer failures or maintenance downtime. CLI command: "lpadmin -p POOL_NAME -v device-uri" to create a printer pool.

In summary, print job queuing and management are essential components of print infrastructure administration, enabling organizations to optimize print system performance, minimize printing costs, and enhance user productivity. By implementing robust print job queuing and management strategies, administrators can streamline print job processing, prioritize printing tasks, and allocate printing resources effectively, ensuring efficient use of printing resources and maintaining high levels of user satisfaction. With the right combination of print management tools, techniques, and best practices, organizations can achieve seamless print job queuing and management, enabling smooth printing operations and maximizing return on investment in print infrastructure.

Chapter 8: Handling User Account Issues

Managing user permissions and access rights is a critical aspect of information security and system administration, essential for protecting sensitive data, safeguarding resources, and ensuring compliance with regulatory requirements. User permissions define the actions and operations that users are allowed to perform on computing resources such as files, folders, applications, and network resources, while access rights determine the level of access granted to users based on their roles, responsibilities, and organizational requirements. Effective management of user permissions and access rights involves defining access control policies, assigning appropriate permissions to users and groups, and implementing security mechanisms to enforce access controls and prevent unauthorized access to sensitive information.

One fundamental aspect of managing user permissions is defining access control lists (ACLs) for files and directories, specifying the permissions granted to users and groups for accessing and modifying resources. ACLs consist of entries that define access permissions for specific users or groups, including read, write, execute, and delete permissions. Administrators can use the "chmod" command on Unix-like systems or the "icacls" command on Windows systems to set ACLs for files and directories, allowing or denying access to users based on their permissions. For example, the command "chmod u+rwx file.txt" grants the owner of the file read, write, and execute permissions.

To simplify user permission management and ensure consistency across multiple files and directories, administrators can create and assign permissions to groups of users with similar roles or responsibilities. By grouping users into logical units based on their job functions or departmental affiliations, administrators can apply consistent access control policies and permissions to all members of the group, streamlining user management and reducing administrative overhead. Group-based permissions allow administrators to assign permissions to groups rather than individual users, making it easier to manage access rights for large numbers of users. CLI command: "chown" (Unix-like systems) or "icacls" (Windows) to change file ownership.

In addition to defining file and directory permissions, administrators can manage user permissions for network resources such as shared folders, printers, and network drives. Network resource permissions are defined using access control lists (ACLs) or permissions settings specific to the network operating system or file sharing protocol used. For example, administrators can use the "net share" command on Windows systems to create shared folders and specify permissions for accessing and modifying shared resources. Similarly, administrators can configure permissions settings for network drives and printers using the administrative tools provided by the network operating system. CLI command: "net share SHARE_NAME=PATH /grant:USER:PERMISSION" to create a shared folder.

To enforce access controls and prevent unauthorized access to sensitive information, administrators can implement authentication mechanisms such as passwords, biometric authentication, or multi-factor authentication (MFA) to verify the identity of users before granting access to resources. Authentication mechanisms require users to provide credentials such as usernames and passwords or biometric data such as fingerprints or facial scans to prove their identity and authenticate themselves to the system. Additionally, administrators can enable MFA to require users to provide multiple forms of identification, such as a password and a one-time passcode sent to their mobile device, to enhance security and mitigate the risk of unauthorized access. CLI command: "passwd" (Unix-like systems) or "net user" (Windows) to manage user passwords.

Furthermore, administrators can implement role-based access control (RBAC) policies to manage user permissions and access rights based on their roles, responsibilities, and job functions within the organization. RBAC assigns users to roles or groups based on their job duties and assigns permissions to roles rather than individual users, allowing administrators to manage access rights centrally and enforce least privilege principles. By defining roles that correspond to specific job functions or organizational roles, administrators can ensure that users have access only to the resources and privileges necessary to perform their duties, minimizing the risk of unauthorized access and data breaches. CLI command: "roleadd" (Unix-like systems) or "New-RoleAssignment" (PowerShell) to create role assignments.

To audit and monitor user permissions and access rights, administrators can implement logging and auditing mechanisms to track user activity, access attempts, and changes to permissions settings. Logging and auditing tools provide administrators with visibility into user actions and events related to permissions management, allowing them to identify suspicious activity, unauthorized access attempts, and compliance violations. By reviewing audit logs and reports regularly, administrators can detect security incidents, investigate potential breaches, and take corrective actions to mitigate risks and strengthen access controls. CLI command: "auditctl" (Unix-like systems) or "auditpol" (Windows) to configure auditing policies.

Moreover, administrators can leverage directory services such as Active Directory (AD) or Lightweight Directory Access Protocol (LDAP) to centralize user management and authentication, streamline user provisioning and deprovisioning, and enforce access controls across multiple systems and applications. Directory services provide a centralized repository for user accounts, groups, and access control policies, allowing administrators to manage user permissions and access rights from a single console or interface. By integrating directory services with other systems and applications, administrators can synchronize user accounts, enforce password policies, and automate user provisioning workflows, reducing administrative overhead and improving security. CLI command: "ldapsearch" (Unix-like systems) or "dsquery" (Windows) to query directory service objects.

In summary, managing user permissions and access rights is a critical aspect of information security and system administration, essential for protecting sensitive data, safeguarding resources, and ensuring compliance with regulatory requirements. By defining access control policies, assigning appropriate permissions to users and groups, and implementing security mechanisms such as authentication and RBAC, administrators can enforce access controls effectively, prevent unauthorized access, and mitigate the risk of security breaches. With robust user permission management practices and access control mechanisms in place, organizations can maintain the confidentiality, integrity, and availability of their information assets and systems, ensuring a secure and productive computing environment.

Password reset procedures are essential components of IT security policies and practices, designed to help users regain access to their accounts in the event of forgotten passwords, compromised credentials, or account lockouts. Effective password reset procedures ensure that users can reset their passwords securely, without compromising the confidentiality and integrity of their accounts or exposing sensitive information to unauthorized individuals. By implementing robust password reset procedures and leveraging security best practices, organizations can maintain the security of their systems and protect against unauthorized access and data breaches.

One common approach to password reset procedures is self-service password reset (SSPR), which allows users to reset their passwords independently without the need for assistance from IT support personnel. SSPR solutions typically involve the use of identity verification mechanisms such as security questions, SMS verification codes, or email-based verification links to authenticate users and validate their identities before allowing them to reset their passwords. Administrators can deploy SSPR solutions either as standalone applications or as integrated features of identity management systems or authentication platforms. For example, Microsoft Azure Active Directory (AAD) provides SSPR capabilities that enable users to reset their passwords via email or SMS verification. CLI command: "Get-MsolUser - UserPrincipalName user@example.com | Set-MsolUserPassword -NewPassword NewPassword - ForceChangePassword $false" to reset a user's password in Azure AD.

Another approach to password reset procedures is manual password reset by IT support personnel, which may be necessary in cases where SSPR solutions are unavailable or user identity verification cannot be completed successfully. Manual password reset procedures typically involve verifying the user's identity through alternate means such as photo identification, employee ID badges, or challenge-response authentication, followed by generating and assigning a temporary password or initiating a password reset process on behalf of the user. IT support personnel must follow strict protocols and procedures to ensure the security and confidentiality of user credentials during manual password reset operations, including verifying the legitimacy of password reset requests, documenting all password reset activities, and enforcing access controls to prevent unauthorized access to sensitive information. CLI command: "net user username newpassword" (Windows) or "passwd username" (Unix-like systems) to reset a user's password manually.

In addition to user-initiated and manual password reset procedures, organizations can implement automated password expiration and rotation policies to enforce regular password changes and mitigate the risk of password-related security incidents such as password guessing attacks or credential theft. Automated password expiration and rotation policies typically involve setting predefined password expiration periods (e.g., 90 days) and enforcing password complexity requirements (e.g., minimum length, character types) to ensure that passwords remain secure and resistant to brute-force attacks. Administrators can use password management tools or identity and access management (IAM) solutions to automate password expiration and rotation processes and enforce compliance with organizational security policies and regulatory requirements. CLI command: "chage -M 90 username" (Unix-like systems) or "net accounts /maxpwage:90" (Windows) to set maximum password age.

Furthermore, organizations can enhance the security of password reset procedures by implementing multi-factor authentication (MFA) mechanisms that require users to provide multiple forms of identification before resetting their passwords. MFA adds an additional layer of security beyond traditional password-based authentication by requiring users to provide something they know (e.g., password) and something they have (e.g., mobile device, security token) or something they are (e.g., fingerprint, facial recognition) to verify their identity and authenticate themselves. By combining multiple authentication factors, MFA strengthens password reset procedures and reduces the risk of unauthorized access resulting from compromised credentials or weak passwords. CLI command: "aws iam create-login-profile --user-name username --password password --password-reset-required" (AWS CLI) to create a login profile with password reset required.

To ensure the effectiveness of password reset procedures and enhance user experience, organizations should provide clear and accessible instructions and guidance for users on how to reset their passwords securely. This may include creating user-friendly self-service password reset portals or web interfaces that guide users through the password reset process step-by-step, provide helpful tips and suggestions for choosing strong passwords, and offer assistance or support options in case of difficulties or questions. Additionally, organizations should educate users on best practices for password management, such as using unique passwords for each account, avoiding common passwords or dictionary words, and enabling additional security features such as two-factor authentication (2FA) or biometric authentication where available. CLI command: "cupsctl WebInterface=yes" to enable the CUPS web interface for accessing printer settings and configuration.

In summary, password reset procedures are essential components of IT security policies and practices, designed to help users regain access to their accounts securely in the event of forgotten passwords, compromised credentials, or account lockouts. By implementing robust password reset procedures and leveraging security best practices such as self-service password reset (SSPR), multi-factor authentication (MFA), and automated password expiration and rotation, organizations can maintain the security of their systems and protect against unauthorized access and data breaches. With clear instructions, user-friendly interfaces, and ongoing user education and awareness programs, organizations can empower users to reset their passwords securely and contribute to the overall security posture of the organization.

Chapter 9: Security Fundamentals for Desktop Support

Recognizing security threats is a crucial skill for individuals and organizations to safeguard their digital assets and sensitive information from various malicious actors and cyber threats. In today's interconnected and digitalized world, the landscape of security threats is constantly evolving, with attackers employing increasingly sophisticated techniques to exploit vulnerabilities and compromise systems. By understanding the different types of security threats and their characteristics, users and organizations can better protect themselves against cyber attacks and mitigate the risks posed by potential security breaches.

One common type of security threat is malware, which encompasses a broad range of malicious software designed to infiltrate systems, steal data, and disrupt operations. Malware includes viruses, worms, trojans, ransomware, spyware, and adware, each with its own unique characteristics and attack vectors. Viruses are self-replicating programs that infect files and spread across systems via infected files or email attachments, while worms are standalone programs that propagate themselves over networks without requiring user interaction. Trojans masquerade as legitimate software to trick users into executing them, granting attackers unauthorized access to systems. Ransomware encrypts files or locks down systems, demanding ransom payments for their release. Spyware and adware track user activities or display unwanted advertisements, compromising privacy and system performance. CLI command: "sudo apt-get install clamav" (Linux) or "Install-Malware -Name 'MalwareName'" (PowerShell) to install malware detection tools.

Phishing is another prevalent security threat that targets users through deceptive emails, messages, or websites to trick them into disclosing sensitive information such as usernames, passwords, or financial details. Phishing attacks often impersonate trusted entities such as banks, social media platforms, or government agencies, exploiting users' trust and familiarity to deceive them into clicking on malicious links or downloading malicious attachments. Spear phishing targets specific individuals or organizations, tailoring the phishing messages to their interests or roles to increase the likelihood of success. Phishing attacks can lead to identity theft, account takeover, or financial loss if users unwittingly divulge their credentials or personal information to attackers. CLI command: "sudo apt-get install opendkim opendkim-tools" (Linux) or "Set-PhishingFilter -Enabled $true" (PowerShell) to enable phishing detection mechanisms.

Social engineering is a tactic commonly used by attackers to manipulate individuals into divulging confidential information or performing actions that compromise security. Social engineering techniques exploit human psychology and emotions such as trust, fear, or curiosity to deceive users and gain unauthorized access to systems or information. Common social engineering techniques include pretexting, where attackers fabricate a scenario or pretext to trick users into providing information or access, and baiting, where attackers lure users into downloading malware or disclosing information by offering tempting rewards or incentives. Social engineering attacks can occur in various forms, including phone calls, emails, text messages, or in-person interactions, making them difficult to detect and mitigate. CLI command: "social-engineer-toolkit" (Linux) or "Invoke-SocialEngineeringAttack -Type Pretexting" (PowerShell) to simulate social engineering attacks for educational purposes.

Another security threat is insider threats, which involve malicious or negligent actions by individuals within an organization that compromise security or pose risks to sensitive information. Insider threats can take various forms, including employees leaking confidential data, intentionally deleting or modifying data, or inadvertently exposing sensitive information through careless or negligent behavior. Insider threats may result from disgruntled employees seeking revenge, employees falling victim to social engineering attacks, or employees lacking awareness of security best practices and policies. Insider threats pose significant challenges for organizations due to the difficulty of detecting and mitigating them without infringing on employees' privacy or undermining trust within the organization. CLI command: "Get-User -Identity username | Disable-UserAccount -Reason 'Security Threat'" (PowerShell) to disable user accounts in response to insider threats.

Denial-of-Service (DoS) and Distributed Denial-of-Service (DDoS) attacks are security threats that aim to disrupt the availability of services or systems by overwhelming them with a high volume of malicious traffic or requests. DoS attacks target individual systems or network resources, such as web servers or routers, by flooding them with traffic or exploiting vulnerabilities to crash or disable them. DDoS attacks involve coordinated efforts by multiple attackers or compromised devices to launch simultaneous attacks from different locations, making them more difficult to mitigate. DoS and DDoS attacks can result in service outages, downtime, or financial losses for organizations, highlighting the importance of implementing robust network defenses and mitigation strategies. CLI command: "sudo iptables -A INPUT -p tcp --dport 80 -j DROP" (Linux) or "Set-NetFirewallRule -DisplayName 'Block-DDoS-Traffic' -Enabled $true" (PowerShell) to block malicious traffic.

Data breaches are security incidents that involve unauthorized access to sensitive information, such as personal data, financial records, or intellectual property, resulting in its theft, disclosure, or manipulation. Data breaches can occur due to various factors, including malware infections, phishing attacks, insider threats, or vulnerabilities in systems or applications. Attackers may exploit data breaches for financial gain, identity theft, corporate espionage, or sabotage, posing significant risks to affected individuals and organizations. Data breaches can have severe consequences, including reputational damage, legal liabilities, regulatory fines, and loss of customer trust. CLI command: "sudo apt-get install ossec-hids" (Linux) or "Install-DataLossPrevention

-Type 'DataBreach'" (PowerShell) to deploy data loss prevention tools.

In summary, recognizing security threats is essential for individuals and organizations to protect themselves against various cyber threats and mitigate the risks posed by potential security breaches. By understanding the characteristics and attack vectors of different types of security threats, users and organizations can implement appropriate security measures, such as malware detection tools, phishing filters, social engineering awareness training, access controls, network defenses, and incident response procedures, to safeguard their digital assets and sensitive information effectively. With proactive threat detection, mitigation strategies, and ongoing security awareness training, individuals and organizations can enhance their security posture and reduce the likelihood of falling victim to cyber attacks.

Implementing basic security measures is essential for individuals and organizations to protect their digital assets, sensitive information, and privacy from various security threats and cyber attacks. Basic security measures encompass a range of practices, tools, and techniques aimed at preventing unauthorized access, detecting and mitigating security risks, and ensuring the confidentiality, integrity, and availability of data and systems. By adopting and implementing basic security measures, users and organizations can establish a strong foundation for cybersecurity and reduce their exposure to security vulnerabilities and risks.

One fundamental aspect of implementing basic security measures is securing user accounts and authentication mechanisms to prevent unauthorized access to systems and data. This includes enforcing strong password policies, such as requiring passwords to be complex, lengthy, and regularly updated, and implementing multi-factor authentication (MFA) to add an extra layer of security beyond passwords. MFA requires users to provide additional forms of identification, such as a one-time passcode sent to their mobile device or a biometric scan, to verify their identity before granting access. CLI command: "passwd" (Unix-like systems) or "Set-LocalUser -Name username -Password NewPassword" (PowerShell) to change a user's password.

Another critical aspect of basic security measures is keeping software and systems up to date by installing security patches and updates promptly. Software vendors regularly release patches and updates to address security vulnerabilities, bugs, and weaknesses discovered in their products, making it essential for users and organizations to apply these patches promptly to minimize the risk of exploitation by attackers. Automated patch management tools and software update mechanisms can streamline the process of identifying and deploying patches across multiple systems and applications, ensuring timely patching and reducing the window of exposure to known security vulnerabilities. CLI command: "sudo apt update && sudo apt upgrade" (Linux) or "wuauclt /detectnow" (Windows) to check for and install updates.

Additionally, implementing network security measures is crucial for protecting data in transit and defending against network-based attacks. This includes deploying firewalls, intrusion detection and prevention systems (IDS/IPS), and virtual private networks (VPNs) to monitor and control network traffic, block malicious activity, and encrypt communications over untrusted networks. Firewalls act as a barrier between internal and external networks, filtering incoming and outgoing traffic based on predefined rules to prevent unauthorized access and protect against known threats. IDS/IPS systems analyze network traffic for signs of suspicious or malicious activity and take automated actions to block or mitigate threats in real-time. VPNs create secure and encrypted connections between remote users and corporate networks, ensuring privacy and confidentiality over public networks. CLI command: "sudo ufw enable" (Linux) or "Enable-WindowsOptionalFeature -Online -FeatureName 'DirectAccess-VPN'" (PowerShell) to enable firewall or VPN features.

Furthermore, implementing data encryption measures helps protect sensitive information from unauthorized access and disclosure, both at rest and in transit. Data encryption involves converting plaintext data into ciphertext using cryptographic algorithms and keys, rendering it unreadable and unintelligible to unauthorized individuals without the appropriate decryption keys. Full-disk encryption (FDE) encrypts the entire storage volume of a device, protecting data stored on disk from unauthorized access if the device is lost or stolen. File and folder encryption encrypts individual files or directories, providing granular control over access to sensitive data. Transport Layer Security (TLS) and Secure Sockets Layer (SSL) protocols encrypt data transmitted over the internet, ensuring confidentiality and integrity during transit. CLI command: "sudo apt-get install cryptsetup" (Linux) or "Add-BitLockerKeyProtector -MountPoint 'C:' - RecoveryPasswordProtector" (PowerShell) to enable disk encryption.

Additionally, implementing security awareness training and education programs for users is essential for promoting a culture of cybersecurity and empowering individuals to recognize and respond to security threats effectively. Security awareness training helps users understand common security risks and threats, recognize phishing attempts, identify suspicious behavior or activity, and follow best practices for protecting sensitive information and maintaining security hygiene. Training programs may include interactive modules, simulated phishing exercises, and knowledge assessments to reinforce learning and ensure that users are equipped with the skills and knowledge needed to protect themselves and the organization from security threats. CLI command: "sudo apt-get install openssh-server" (Linux) or "Install-WindowsFeature -Name RSAT-ADDS" (PowerShell) to install security training tools or Active Directory features.

Moreover, implementing regular security audits, assessments, and vulnerability scans is essential for

identifying and addressing security weaknesses and gaps in systems, applications, and processes. Security audits involve reviewing and analyzing security controls, policies, and procedures to ensure compliance with regulatory requirements and industry best practices. Vulnerability scans and assessments involve scanning systems and networks for known vulnerabilities, misconfigurations, or weaknesses that could be exploited by attackers. By conducting regular security audits and vulnerability scans, organizations can proactively identify and remediate security issues before they are exploited by attackers, reducing the risk of security breaches and data loss. CLI command: "lynis audit system" (Linux) or "Invoke-WebRequest -Uri 'https://www.example.com/vulnerability-scan'"
(PowerShell) to perform security audits or vulnerability scans.

In summary, implementing basic security measures is essential for individuals and organizations to protect their digital assets, sensitive information, and privacy from various security threats and cyber attacks. By adopting and implementing robust security practices, such as securing user accounts, keeping software up to date, deploying network security measures, encrypting data, providing security awareness training, and conducting regular

Chapter 10: Remote Desktop Assistance Techniques

Remote Desktop Protocol (RDP) is a proprietary protocol developed by Microsoft that enables users to connect to and interact with remote computers or virtual desktops over a network connection. RDP allows users to access the graphical user interface (GUI) of a remote computer and control it as if they were physically present at the remote location. This capability facilitates remote administration, troubleshooting, software development, and remote access to desktop applications and resources, making it a valuable tool for individuals and organizations seeking to enhance productivity, collaboration, and flexibility in their computing environments.

RDP operates on Transmission Control Protocol (TCP) port 3389 by default and uses a client-server model, where the client application, known as the Remote Desktop Client or Remote Desktop Connection (RDC), initiates a connection to the remote computer, also known as the Remote Desktop Host or Remote Desktop Server. Once the connection is established, the client sends input from the user, such as keyboard and mouse actions, to the remote computer, and the remote computer transmits the graphical output back to the client, allowing the user to view and interact with the remote desktop environment. CLI command: "mstsc" (Windows) or "xfreerdp" (Linux) to launch the Remote Desktop Client.

One of the key features of RDP is its support for remote display protocols, which enable efficient transmission of graphical data between the client and server over low-bandwidth or high-latency network connections. RDP employs various compression and encoding techniques to minimize the amount of data transmitted over the network and optimize performance, responsiveness, and image quality during remote desktop sessions. These protocols include RemoteFX, which enhances graphics rendering and multimedia playback, and Network Level Authentication (NLA), which authenticates users before establishing a remote desktop connection to prevent unauthorized access. CLI command: "Set-ItemProperty -Path 'HKLM:\System\CurrentControlSet\Control\Terminal Server\WinStations\RDP-Tcp' -Name 'UserAuthentication' -Value 1" (PowerShell) to enable Network Level Authentication.

In addition to facilitating remote desktop access, RDP supports various advanced features and functionalities to enhance security, usability, and productivity. These features include remote audio and video redirection, which allows users to play multimedia content on the remote computer and stream the audio and video output to their local device, ensuring a seamless multimedia experience during remote desktop sessions. RDP also supports clipboard redirection, enabling users to copy and paste text, images, and files between the local and remote desktop environments, facilitating data transfer and collaboration across remote locations. CLI command: "gpedit.msc" (Windows) or "sudo apt-get install xrdp" (Linux) to configure RDP settings and features.

Moreover, RDP offers support for remote printing, enabling users to print documents and files from the remote desktop environment to local printers connected to their client devices. RDP printer redirection redirects print jobs from the remote computer to the client device, where they are rendered and printed using the local printer drivers and settings, ensuring compatibility and consistency with the user's printing environment. This feature enhances productivity and convenience for users who need to print documents or files while working remotely, eliminating the need to transfer files or documents between the remote and local environments for printing. CLI command: "cscript %systemroot%\system32\prndrvr.vbs -a -m 'printer driver' -i 'inf file'" (Windows) to install printer drivers.

Furthermore, RDP supports session persistence and mobility, allowing users to disconnect from remote desktop sessions without logging off, preserving their session state and application state on the remote computer. When users reconnect to the same session later, they can resume their work exactly where they left off, with all open applications, documents, and settings intact. This feature is particularly useful for mobile users who need to access their desktop environments from multiple locations or devices, as it enables seamless continuity and productivity across different computing environments. CLI command:

"qwinsta" (Windows) or "xrdp-sesman --list" (Linux) to list active RDP sessions.

However, despite its numerous benefits and capabilities, RDP also poses security risks and vulnerabilities if not configured and managed properly. RDP is a common target for cyber attackers seeking to exploit misconfigured or unsecured RDP services to gain unauthorized access to systems and networks. Attackers may use brute-force attacks, credential stuffing attacks, or exploits targeting RDP vulnerabilities to compromise remote desktop services and infiltrate corporate networks, steal sensitive information, or deploy ransomware. To mitigate these risks, organizations should implement best practices for securing RDP, such as disabling RDP access for unnecessary users or accounts, enabling Network Level Authentication (NLA), implementing strong password policies, and regularly updating and patching RDP servers and client devices. CLI command: "Set-ItemProperty -Path 'HKLM:\System\CurrentControlSet\Control\Terminal Server\WinStations\RDP-Tcp' -Name 'fDenyTSConnections' -Value 1" (PowerShell) to disable RDP access.

In summary, Remote Desktop Protocol (RDP) is a powerful and versatile technology that enables users to access and control remote computers or virtual desktops over a network connection. RDP provides essential features and functionalities for remote administration, troubleshooting, collaboration, and productivity, enhancing flexibility and efficiency in modern computing environments. By understanding the capabilities, features, and security considerations of RDP, users and organizations can leverage this technology effectively while mitigating the associated risks and vulnerabilities to ensure secure and productive remote desktop experiences.

Troubleshooting remote access connectivity issues is a critical skill for IT professionals tasked with managing and maintaining remote access infrastructure and ensuring uninterrupted access to resources for remote users. Remote access connectivity issues can arise due to various factors, including network configuration errors, firewall restrictions, authentication problems, and software conflicts, among others. Effective troubleshooting requires a systematic approach, thorough understanding of networking principles, and familiarity with remote access technologies and protocols to identify and resolve connectivity issues promptly and minimize disruption to users.

One common cause of remote access connectivity issues is network configuration errors, such as incorrect IP addressing, subnetting, or routing settings, which can prevent remote users from establishing connections to network resources. To troubleshoot network configuration issues, IT professionals can use diagnostic tools such as ping, traceroute, and ipconfig (Windows) or ifconfig (Linux) to verify network connectivity, identify network devices and routes, and check IP configuration settings on client devices and network infrastructure. These tools help pinpoint network misconfigurations or connectivity problems, enabling IT professionals to correct them and restore remote access connectivity. Command example: "ping hostname" to check connectivity to a remote host.

Another common cause of remote access connectivity issues is firewall restrictions or port blocking, which can prevent incoming or outgoing traffic necessary for remote access protocols from reaching their destinations. Firewalls, both at the network perimeter and on client devices, may block specific ports or protocols used by remote access applications, such as Remote Desktop Protocol (RDP), Virtual Private Network (VPN), or Secure Shell (SSH), resulting in connection failures or timeouts. To troubleshoot firewall issues, IT professionals can use port scanning tools such as nmap to identify open, closed, or filtered ports on remote hosts and network devices, allowing them to adjust firewall rules or port forwarding settings as needed to allow traffic for remote access protocols. Command example: "nmap -p 3389 hostname" to scan for open ports.

Authentication problems can also cause remote access connectivity issues, particularly when users encounter errors during the authentication process or fail to authenticate successfully due to incorrect credentials or account permissions. Authentication failures may occur due to misconfigured authentication settings, expired or disabled user accounts, or mismatched authentication protocols between the client and server. To troubleshoot authentication issues, IT professionals can check authentication logs, event logs, or security logs on authentication servers or remote access devices to identify failed login attempts, authentication errors, or account lockouts, allowing them to diagnose and resolve authentication-related issues promptly. Command example: "tail -f /var/log/auth.log" to monitor authentication logs.

Software conflicts or compatibility issues can also interfere with remote access connectivity, particularly when users encounter errors or compatibility warnings when using remote access applications or protocols. Software conflicts may arise due to incompatible software versions, outdated drivers, or conflicting applications running on client devices or remote hosts, leading to connectivity problems or application crashes. To troubleshoot software conflicts, IT professionals can update or reinstall remote access applications, drivers, or dependencies on client devices, ensuring compatibility with the remote access infrastructure and resolving any conflicts that may prevent successful connections. Command example: "sudo apt-get update && sudo apt-get install --reinstall rdp-client" to reinstall the Remote Desktop Protocol (RDP) client.

Additionally, bandwidth limitations or network congestion can affect remote access connectivity, particularly in environments with limited bandwidth or high network traffic volume, leading to slow or intermittent connections, packet loss, or latency issues. Bandwidth limitations may occur due to network congestion, insufficient bandwidth capacity, or bandwidth throttling policies implemented by Internet service providers (ISPs) or network administrators. To troubleshoot bandwidth-related issues, IT professionals can use network monitoring tools such as Wireshark or

SNMP (Simple Network Management Protocol) to analyze network traffic patterns, monitor bandwidth utilization, and identify congestion points or bottlenecks affecting remote access performance. Command example: "sudo apt-get install wireshark" to install Wireshark for network traffic analysis.

Moreover, hardware failures or malfunctions can disrupt remote access connectivity, particularly when network devices, routers, switches, or modems experience hardware failures or power outages that affect network connectivity or device operation. Hardware failures may manifest as connectivity errors, device unresponsiveness, or intermittent network connectivity issues, requiring troubleshooting and hardware replacement to restore normal operation. To troubleshoot hardware failures, IT professionals can perform hardware diagnostics, check device status indicators, and verify hardware connections and power supplies to identify faulty components or hardware-related issues affecting remote access connectivity. Command example: "dmesg | grep error" to check for hardware error messages.

Furthermore, configuration errors or misconfigurations in remote access infrastructure, such as VPN servers, remote desktop hosts, or terminal servers, can cause connectivity issues for remote users attempting to establish connections to network resources. Configuration errors may involve incorrect settings, permissions, or access controls configured on remote access devices or servers, preventing users from accessing resources or establishing connections. To troubleshoot configuration issues, IT professionals can review configuration settings, logs, or diagnostic information on remote access devices or servers to identify misconfigurations or inconsistencies and correct them to restore connectivity. Command example: "cat /etc/openvpn/server.conf" to view OpenVPN server configuration settings.

In summary, troubleshooting remote access connectivity issues requires a systematic approach, thorough understanding of networking principles, and familiarity with remote access technologies and protocols to identify and resolve connectivity problems promptly.

BOOK 2
MASTERING NETWORK BASICS FUNDAMENTAL
TECHNIQUES FOR DESKTOP SUPPORT

ROB BOTWRIGHT

Chapter 1: Introduction to Computer Networks

The evolution of networking technologies has been a remarkable journey marked by significant advancements and innovations that have revolutionized the way individuals and organizations communicate, collaborate, and exchange information. From the early days of simple point-to-point connections to the complex, interconnected global networks of today, networking technologies have continually evolved to meet the growing demands for connectivity, bandwidth, speed, and reliability in an increasingly digital world.

The evolution of networking technologies can be traced back to the early 1960s with the development of the Advanced Research Projects Agency Network (ARPANET), the precursor to the modern Internet. ARPANET was designed to facilitate communication and resource sharing among researchers and scientists at various institutions, laying the foundation for packet-switched networks and the TCP/IP protocol suite that form the basis of today's Internet. ARPANET introduced concepts such as packet switching, which enabled data to be broken down into smaller packets for more efficient transmission across network links, and distributed network architecture, which allowed multiple interconnected nodes to communicate and share resources. Command example: "ping" to test network connectivity and latency.

In the 1980s and 1990s, the Internet expanded rapidly with the development of new networking technologies and protocols that further enhanced its capabilities and reach. The introduction of Ethernet, a widely used networking technology for local area networks (LANs), enabled high-speed data transmission over copper and fiber optic cables, paving the way for the proliferation of LANs in homes, offices, and academic institutions. Ethernet's scalability, reliability, and cost-effectiveness made it the de facto standard for network connectivity, enabling the seamless integration of computers, printers, servers, and other networked devices into unified network environments. Command example: "ifconfig" (Linux) or "ipconfig" (Windows) to view network interface configuration.

During this period, the Internet Protocol version 4 (IPv4) became the dominant networking protocol for routing and addressing data packets across interconnected networks. IPv4 introduced the concept of IP addressing, assigning unique numerical addresses to devices connected to a network to facilitate data communication and routing. However, as the Internet continued to grow, the limited address space of IPv4 (approximately 4.3 billion addresses) became increasingly strained, leading to the development of IPv6 as the next-generation Internet protocol. IPv6 offers a vastly expanded address space (approximately 340 undecillion addresses) and improved features such as built-in security and support for mobile devices, IoT (Internet of Things) devices, and emerging networking technologies. Command example: "ip addr add <IPv6 address>" to assign an IPv6 address to a network interface.

The emergence of wireless networking technologies in the late 20th century marked another significant milestone in the evolution of networking. Wi-Fi, based on the IEEE 802.11 standards, enabled wireless communication between devices over short distances, eliminating the need for physical cables and enabling mobility and flexibility in network connectivity. Wi-Fi technology has since become ubiquitous, powering wireless networks in homes, businesses, public spaces, and mobile devices worldwide, enabling seamless connectivity and Internet access across a wide range of devices and environments. Command example: "iwconfig" (Linux) or "netsh wlan show interfaces" (Windows) to view wireless interface configuration.

Furthermore, the advent of broadband Internet access technologies, such as Digital Subscriber Line (DSL), cable modem, and fiber optic broadband, has transformed the way people access and consume digital content and services online. Broadband Internet offers high-speed, always-on connectivity, enabling faster downloads, streaming, and real-time communication over the Internet. These technologies have fueled the growth of multimedia content, cloud computing, online gaming, and streaming services, driving innovation and economic growth in the digital economy. Command example: "ip route show" to display the routing table.

In recent years, the rise of cloud computing and virtualization technologies has reshaped the networking landscape, ushering in a new era of software-defined networking (SDN) and network virtualization. SDN decouples network control and forwarding functions, enabling centralized management and programmability of network infrastructure through software-based controllers. Network virtualization abstracts physical network hardware and resources, creating virtual networks that are independent of underlying hardware and topology, providing flexibility, scalability, and agility in network deployment and management. Command example: "sudo apt-get install openvswitch" to install Open vSwitch for software-defined networking.

Moreover, the Internet of Things (IoT) has emerged as a transformative force in networking, connecting billions of smart devices, sensors, and objects to the Internet and enabling new applications and services in diverse domains such as healthcare, transportation, agriculture, and smart cities. IoT networks leverage a variety of wireless communication technologies, including Bluetooth, Zigbee, LoRaWAN, and cellular networks, to enable communication and data exchange between connected devices and cloud-based platforms. These networks enable real-time monitoring, control, and automation of physical objects and processes, leading to improved efficiency, productivity, and quality of life. Command example: "sudo apt-get install mosquitto" to install MQTT broker for IoT communication.

Looking ahead, the evolution of networking technologies is expected to continue at a rapid pace, driven by advancements in areas such as 5G wireless technology, edge computing, artificial intelligence, and quantum networking. 5G promises to deliver ultra-fast, low-latency wireless connectivity, enabling new applications and services such as autonomous vehicles, augmented reality, and remote surgery. Edge computing extends the capabilities of cloud computing to the network edge, enabling real-time processing and analysis of data closer to the source, reducing latency and bandwidth requirements. Artificial intelligence (AI) and machine learning (ML) are being applied to optimize network performance, security, and efficiency, automating network management tasks and predicting and mitigating network failures and security threats. Quantum networking explores the use of quantum mechanics principles to develop secure communication protocols and quantum computing algorithms that leverage quantum entanglement and superposition to perform complex calculations and data processing tasks. Command example: "sudo apt-get install quantum-networking" (hypothetical command for future quantum networking package installation).

In summary, the evolution of networking technologies has been characterized by continuous innovation and advancement, driven by the growing demand for connectivity, bandwidth, speed, and reliability in an increasingly digital and interconnected world. From the early days of ARPANET and Ethernet to the emergence of wireless networking, broadband Internet, cloud computing, SDN, IoT, and beyond, networking technologies have transformed the way we communicate, collaborate, and conduct business, shaping the future of connectivity and digital transformation. As we continue to push the boundaries of what is possible in networking, the next frontier of innovation promises to unlock new possibilities and opportunities for connectivity, intelligence, and collaboration in the digital age.

In understanding computer networks, it's crucial to grasp the fundamental components that make up their architecture and functionality. These components form the backbone of networks, enabling communication and data exchange between devices, systems, and users. From network devices to cabling infrastructure and protocols, each component plays a vital role in ensuring the smooth operation and connectivity of modern networks.

At the core of any network are the devices that facilitate communication and data transfer. These devices include routers, switches, hubs, and access points, each serving a specific purpose in network connectivity and management. Routers are responsible for forwarding data packets between different networks, determining the optimal path for data transmission based on routing tables and network protocols. Command example: "show ip route" to display the router's routing table.

Switches, on the other hand, operate at the data link layer (Layer 2) of the OSI model and are used to connect devices within the same network, such as computers, printers, and servers. Switches use MAC addresses to forward data packets to the appropriate destination device, improving network efficiency and reducing collisions compared to traditional hub-based networks. Command example: "show mac address-table" to view the switch's MAC address table.

Hubs, although less common in modern networks, serve a similar function to switches but operate at the physical layer (Layer 1) of the OSI model. Unlike switches, hubs broadcast data packets to all connected devices, resulting in lower network efficiency and increased collisions. Access points, also known as wireless access points (WAPs), enable wireless connectivity for devices, allowing them to connect to a wired network infrastructure via Wi-Fi. Command example: "show interfaces" to view the hub's connected interfaces.

Another essential component of network infrastructure is the cabling system, which provides the physical medium for data transmission between network devices. Common types of network cables include twisted pair (e.g., Ethernet), coaxial, and fiber optic cables, each offering different performance characteristics, bandwidth capabilities, and transmission distances. Twisted pair cables, such as Cat5e or Cat6, are widely used for Ethernet networking due to their affordability, flexibility, and ease of installation. Coaxial cables are commonly used for cable television (CATV) and broadband Internet connections, while fiber optic cables offer high-speed data transmission over long distances and immunity to electromagnetic interference (EMI). Command example: "ifconfig" (Linux) or "ipconfig" (Windows) to view network interface configuration.

Protocols are another critical component of network communication, defining the rules and conventions for data exchange between devices and systems. TCP/IP (Transmission Control Protocol/Internet Protocol) is the foundation of modern networking, providing a suite of protocols for packet-based communication over interconnected networks. TCP (Transmission Control Protocol) ensures reliable, connection-oriented data transmission, while IP (Internet Protocol) handles addressing, routing, and packet delivery between network devices. Command example: "netstat" to display network statistics and active connections.

Ethernet is another essential protocol in computer networking, governing how devices communicate within the same local area network (LAN). Ethernet uses a set of standards defined by the IEEE (Institute of Electrical and Electronics Engineers), such as IEEE 802.3, to specify data framing, addressing, and collision detection mechanisms. Other notable protocols include ARP (Address Resolution Protocol) for mapping IP addresses to MAC addresses, ICMP (Internet Control Message Protocol) for network troubleshooting and diagnostics, and DHCP (Dynamic Host Configuration Protocol) for automated IP address assignment to network devices. Command example: "arp -a" to display the ARP cache.

Network addressing is a fundamental concept in networking, enabling devices to identify and communicate with each other on a network. IP addresses, assigned to devices using either IPv4 (Internet Protocol version 4) or IPv6 (Internet Protocol version 6), serve as unique identifiers for network interfaces, allowing data packets to be routed across networks. IPv4 addresses consist of 32 bits, expressed in four octets separated by dots (e.g., 192.168.1.1), while IPv6 addresses are 128 bits long, represented in hexadecimal format (e.g., 2001:0db8:85a3:0000:0000:8a2e:0370:7334).

Command example: "ipconfig /all" (Windows) or "ifconfig -a" (Linux) to display IP configuration details.

Security is a critical consideration in network design and operation, with various security measures and mechanisms implemented to protect network resources and data from unauthorized access and malicious attacks. Firewalls, intrusion detection systems (IDS), and intrusion prevention systems (IPS) are essential network security appliances that monitor and control incoming and outgoing network traffic, filtering packets based on predefined security rules and policies. VPNs (Virtual Private Networks) encrypt network traffic over public networks, ensuring confidentiality and data integrity for remote users accessing corporate resources. Command example: "iptables" (Linux) or "netsh advfirewall firewall" (Windows) to configure firewall rules.

Finally, network management tools and protocols are essential for monitoring, troubleshooting, and optimizing network performance and reliability. SNMP (Simple Network Management Protocol) is a widely used network management protocol that enables centralized monitoring and management of network devices and resources. SNMP-enabled devices, such as routers, switches, and servers, expose management information via SNMP agents, allowing network administrators to collect and analyze performance data, configure devices remotely, and receive alerts and notifications about network events. Command example:

"snmpwalk" to retrieve SNMP information from network devices.

In summary, understanding the basic components of computer networks is essential for anyone involved in designing, deploying, or managing network infrastructure. From network devices and cabling to protocols, addressing, security, and management tools, each component plays a crucial role in ensuring the functionality, performance, and security of modern networks. By mastering these fundamental concepts and technologies, network professionals can build robust, scalable, and resilient networks that meet the evolving needs of users and organizations in today's interconnected world.

Chapter 2: Understanding Network Topologies

Network topologies represent the physical or logical layout of interconnected devices in a computer network, defining how devices are connected and how data flows between them. Understanding common network topologies is essential for network engineers and administrators tasked with designing, implementing, and managing network infrastructure to meet the connectivity needs of users and applications. From traditional bus and star topologies to modern mesh and hybrid topologies, each topology has its characteristics, advantages, and limitations, influencing network performance, scalability, and fault tolerance.

One of the simplest and oldest network topologies is the bus topology, where all devices are connected to a single shared communication medium, such as a coaxial cable or Ethernet cable. In a bus topology, data transmitted by one device is received by all other devices on the network, with each device filtering out packets addressed to it. Bus topologies are easy to implement and cost-effective, making them suitable for small networks with few devices. However, bus topologies are prone to collisions and network congestion, as all devices share the same communication channel. Command example: "ipconfig" (Windows) or "ifconfig" (Linux) to view network interface configuration.

The star topology is another common network topology, characterized by a central hub or switch that serves as the focal point for connecting individual devices. In a star topology, each device is connected directly to the central hub or switch, forming a star-shaped configuration. Data transmitted by one device is sent to the central hub or switch, which then forwards the data to the appropriate destination device. Star topologies offer better performance and fault isolation compared to bus topologies, as a single device failure does not affect the entire network. However, star topologies require more cabling and infrastructure than bus topologies, making them more expensive to deploy and manage. Command example: "show cdp neighbors" to display directly connected devices on a Cisco switch.

A variation of the star topology is the extended star or hierarchical topology, which introduces additional layers of switches or hubs to accommodate larger networks with multiple subnetworks or departments. In a hierarchical topology, access switches connect end-user devices, such as computers and printers, to distribution switches, which aggregate traffic from multiple access switches and connect them to the core switches or routers. Core switches or routers provide high-speed connectivity between different parts of the network and serve as the backbone for interconnecting multiple subnetworks. Hierarchical topologies offer scalability, flexibility, and simplified network management, making them suitable for medium to large enterprise networks. Command example: "show spanning-tree" to display Spanning Tree Protocol (STP) information on Cisco switches.

Mesh topologies represent a more robust and fault-tolerant approach to network design, where each device is connected to every other device in the network, forming a fully interconnected mesh of links. Mesh topologies can be either full mesh or partial mesh, depending on the degree of connectivity between devices. In a full mesh topology, every device is connected to every other device, providing redundant paths and fault tolerance, but requiring a large number of links and ports. In a partial mesh topology, only select devices are interconnected, reducing the number of links and ports required while still providing some degree of redundancy and fault tolerance. Mesh topologies are commonly used in critical infrastructure networks, such as telecommunications and data centers, where high availability and reliability are paramount. Command example: "traceroute" to trace the route packets take through the network.

Ring topologies are characterized by a circular arrangement of devices, where each device is connected to exactly two other devices, forming a closed-loop configuration. Data transmitted by one device travels around the ring until it reaches its destination device, with each device regenerating and forwarding the data to the next device in the ring. Ring topologies offer simplicity and low implementation cost but suffer from limited scalability and fault tolerance, as a single device failure can disrupt the entire network. Token Ring and Fiber Distributed Data Interface (FDDI) are examples of ring topologies commonly used in the past but have largely been replaced by more robust and scalable network technologies. Command example: "show interfaces ring" to display interface status on devices in a ring topology.

Hybrid topologies combine two or more different network topologies to create a customized network architecture that meets specific requirements and objectives. Hybrid topologies leverage the strengths of each topology while mitigating their weaknesses, allowing for greater flexibility, scalability, and fault tolerance. For example, a hybrid topology may combine a star topology for local connectivity within departments or branches with a mesh topology for backbone connectivity between sites, providing redundancy and high availability. Hybrid topologies are commonly used in complex enterprise networks and distributed systems, where diverse connectivity requirements must be addressed. Command example: "show ip route" to display routing information on devices in a hybrid topology.

In summary, exploring common network topologies provides valuable insights into the design, implementation, and management of computer networks, enabling network engineers and administrators to make informed decisions about network architecture and infrastructure. Whether deploying a simple bus or star topology for a small office network or designing a complex mesh or hybrid topology for a large enterprise network, understanding the characteristics, advantages, and limitations of each topology is essential for building reliable, scalable, and efficient networks that meet the evolving needs of users and applications in today's digital age.

When designing and implementing a computer network, selecting the appropriate topology is crucial for ensuring optimal performance, scalability, and reliability. Each network topology comes with its own set of advantages and disadvantages, making it essential to weigh the pros and cons carefully to determine the best fit for a specific environment or use case. By comparing different topologies based on their characteristics, features, and suitability for various applications, network designers can make informed decisions to meet the requirements and objectives of their network deployments.

One of the most common network topologies is the star topology, characterized by a central switch or hub that serves as the focal point for connecting all devices in the network. In a star topology, each device is directly connected to the central switch or hub, enabling easy scalability and straightforward troubleshooting. Command example: "show cdp neighbors" to display directly connected devices on a Cisco switch. However, the star topology relies heavily on the central switch or hub, making it a single point of failure. If the central device fails, the entire network may become inaccessible.

In contrast, the bus topology is a simple and cost-effective network layout in which all devices are connected to a single shared communication medium, such as a coaxial cable. In a bus topology, data is transmitted in both directions along the bus, with devices receiving data packets intended for them based on their unique addresses. Command example: "netstat -i" to view network interfaces on a Linux system. The bus topology offers easy scalability and flexibility for adding or removing devices. However, it is susceptible to signal degradation and collisions, especially as the network grows larger, leading to decreased performance and reliability.

Another common network topology is the ring topology, where each device is connected to exactly two other devices, forming a closed loop or ring. In a ring topology, data packets circulate around the ring in a sequential manner until they reach their destination. Command example: "show interface ring" to display interface status on a Cisco router. The ring topology provides equal access to network resources and supports bidirectional communication. However, it is vulnerable to single point failures, as a break in the ring can disrupt network connectivity for all devices.

Mesh topology, on the other hand, offers the highest level of redundancy and fault tolerance by providing multiple paths between devices. In a full mesh topology, every device is connected to every other device, ensuring that if one link fails, alternative paths are available for data transmission. Command example: "traceroute" to trace the path packets take through a network. Mesh topology is highly resilient and can withstand link failures without affecting network performance. However, it is costly and complex to implement, requiring a large number of physical connections and extensive cabling infrastructure.

Hybrid topologies combine elements of different topologies to achieve a balance between cost, performance, and scalability. For example, a hybrid topology may incorporate a combination of star, bus, and ring topologies to meet specific requirements. Command example: "show spanning-tree" to display Spanning Tree Protocol (STP) information on a switch. Hybrid topologies offer flexibility and customization options, allowing network designers to tailor the network layout to suit the needs of their organization. However, they can be challenging to manage and troubleshoot due to their complexity and diversity of components.

When comparing topology advantages and disadvantages, it's essential to consider factors such as scalability, reliability, performance, cost, and ease of management. While some topologies may excel in certain areas, they may fall short in others, necessitating trade-offs and compromises to achieve the desired balance. By evaluating the strengths and weaknesses of each topology against specific requirements and objectives, network designers can make informed decisions to design resilient, efficient, and cost-effective networks that meet the needs of their organization.

In summary, the choice of network topology plays a crucial role in determining the overall performance, reliability, and scalability of a computer network. Each topology has its own set of advantages and disadvantages, making it essential for network designers to carefully evaluate and compare different options based on specific requirements and objectives. By considering factors such as fault tolerance, scalability, cost, and ease of management, network designers can select the most suitable topology to meet the needs of their organization and ensure the success of their network deployments.

Chapter 3: OSI Model Demystified

Understanding the OSI (Open Systems Interconnection) model is essential for comprehending how network protocols and communication work within computer networks. The OSI model provides a conceptual framework for understanding the interactions between different network components and protocols, dividing the communication process into seven distinct layers. Each layer performs specific functions and interacts with adjacent layers to facilitate end-to-end communication between devices. By breaking down the OSI model layers and examining their roles and responsibilities, network professionals can gain insights into how data is transmitted, routed, and processed across networks.

The OSI model consists of seven layers, each with its own unique functions and characteristics. The bottom layer, Layer 1 or the Physical layer, deals with the physical transmission of data over the network medium. This layer defines the physical characteristics of the transmission medium, including the type of cables, connectors, and signaling methods used to transmit data. Command example: "ip link show" to display network interface information. Layer 1 also handles tasks such as data encoding, modulation, and transmission timing, ensuring that bits are transmitted reliably between devices.

Above the Physical layer is Layer 2, known as the Data Link layer. This layer is responsible for providing error-free transmission of data frames between adjacent network devices, such as switches and network interface cards (NICs). The Data Link layer encapsulates data into frames, adds source and destination MAC addresses, and performs error detection and correction using techniques like CRC (Cyclic Redundancy Check). Command example: "show interface status" to display interface status on a Cisco switch. Layer 2 also manages access to the physical medium through protocols like Ethernet and Wi-Fi.

Moving up the OSI model, Layer 3 is the Network layer, which focuses on the logical addressing, routing, and forwarding of data packets between different networks. The Network layer adds network layer addresses (e.g., IP addresses) to data packets, allowing them to be routed across interconnected networks. Command example: "route print" to display the routing table on a Windows system. Layer 3 devices, such as routers, use routing algorithms and protocols like IP and ICMP to determine the best path for data transmission based on network topology and destination address.

Layer 4, the Transport layer, provides end-to-end communication and error recovery mechanisms between host devices. This layer ensures the reliable delivery of data by segmenting, sequencing, and reassembling data packets transmitted between applications. The Transport layer also performs flow control and congestion avoidance to prevent network congestion and packet loss. Command example: "netstat -s" to display network statistics on a Linux system. Layer 4 protocols, such as TCP (Transmission

Control Protocol) and UDP (User Datagram Protocol), govern communication between applications and manage data transfer sessions.

Above the Transport layer is Layer 5, the Session layer, which establishes, maintains, and terminates communication sessions between devices. This layer manages session synchronization, checkpointing, and recovery mechanisms to ensure that data exchange between applications occurs smoothly and efficiently. Command example: "ss" to display socket statistics on a Linux system. Layer 5 protocols, such as SSH (Secure Shell) and TLS (Transport Layer Security), provide secure and reliable session-based communication for applications.

Layer 6, the Presentation layer, is responsible for data translation, encryption, and compression to ensure compatibility between different systems and applications. This layer formats data into a standard syntax and encoding format to facilitate interoperability and data exchange. Command example: "openssl enc -aes-256-cbc" to encrypt data using OpenSSL. Layer 6 protocols, such as MIME (Multipurpose Internet Mail Extensions) and JPEG (Joint Photographic Experts Group), handle data representation and transformation tasks.

At the top of the OSI model is Layer 7, the Application layer, which interacts directly with end-user applications and services. This layer provides network services and interfaces for applications to access network resources, such as email, web browsing, file transfer, and remote access. Command example: "curl" to transfer data from or to a server using various protocols. Layer 7 protocols, such as HTTP (Hypertext Transfer Protocol) and FTP (File Transfer Protocol), enable communication and data exchange between applications running on different devices.

By understanding the breakdown of OSI model layers and their respective functions, network professionals can troubleshoot network issues, design efficient network architectures, and implement effective communication protocols. Each layer plays a vital role in the end-to-end communication process, ensuring that data is transmitted, routed, and delivered reliably between devices and applications. As networks continue to evolve and grow in complexity, a solid understanding of the OSI model remains essential for building resilient, scalable, and secure network infrastructures.

In understanding how data is transmitted across computer networks, it's crucial to delve into the role of each OSI (Open Systems Interconnection) model layer. The OSI model provides a conceptual framework for comprehending the various stages and processes involved in transmitting data between devices. Each layer of the OSI model performs specific functions that contribute to the end-to-end communication process, ensuring that data is transmitted efficiently, reliably, and securely across networks. By exploring the role of each OSI layer in data transmission, network professionals can gain insights into the inner workings of network communication and troubleshoot issues effectively.

Starting at the bottom of the OSI model is Layer 1, also known as the Physical layer. The primary role of the Physical layer is to define the physical characteristics of the communication medium and facilitate the transmission of raw binary data between devices. This layer deals with hardware components such as cables, connectors, and network interface cards (NICs), ensuring that data signals are transmitted accurately across the network medium. Command example: "ifconfig" to display network interface configuration details.

Layer 2, the Data Link layer, builds upon the Physical layer by providing error-free transmission of data frames between directly connected devices. One of the key functions of the Data Link layer is to encapsulate data into frames and add necessary control information, such as source and destination MAC addresses. Additionally, this layer performs error detection and correction using techniques like CRC (Cyclic Redundancy Check) to ensure data integrity during transmission. Command example: "show interface" to display interface status on a router or switch.

Moving up the OSI model, Layer 3 is the Network layer, which focuses on logical addressing, routing, and forwarding of data packets between different networks. The Network layer adds network layer addresses (e.g., IP addresses) to data packets, allowing them to be routed across interconnected networks. This layer employs routing algorithms and protocols to determine the optimal path for data transmission based on network topology and destination address. Command example: "traceroute" to trace the path packets take through a network.

Layer 4, the Transport layer, provides end-to-end communication and error recovery mechanisms between host devices. This layer ensures the reliable delivery of data by segmenting, sequencing, and reassembling data packets transmitted between applications. Additionally, the Transport layer performs flow control and congestion avoidance to prevent network congestion and packet loss. Command example: "netstat" to display network statistics and active connections.

Above the Transport layer is Layer 5, the Session layer, which establishes, maintains, and terminates communication sessions between devices. This layer manages session synchronization, checkpointing, and recovery mechanisms to ensure that data exchange between applications occurs smoothly and efficiently. Layer 5 protocols, such as SSH (Secure Shell) and TLS (Transport Layer Security), provide secure and reliable session-based communication for applications.

Layer 6, the Presentation layer, is responsible for data translation, encryption, and compression to ensure compatibility between different systems and applications. This layer formats data into a standard syntax and encoding format to facilitate interoperability and data exchange. Layer 6 protocols, such as MIME (Multipurpose Internet Mail Extensions) and JPEG (Joint Photographic Experts Group), handle data representation and transformation tasks.

At the top of the OSI model is Layer 7, the Application layer, which interacts directly with end-user applications and services. This layer provides network services and interfaces for applications to access network resources, such as email, web browsing, file transfer, and remote access. Layer 7 protocols, such as HTTP (Hypertext Transfer Protocol) and FTP (File Transfer Protocol), enable communication and data exchange between applications running on different devices.

In summary, each OSI layer plays a crucial role in the transmission of data across computer networks, from defining the physical characteristics of the communication medium to facilitating end-to-end communication between applications. By understanding the functions and responsibilities of each OSI layer, network professionals can diagnose network issues, design efficient network architectures, and implement effective communication protocols. As networks continue to evolve and grow in complexity, a solid understanding of the role of each OSI layer remains essential for building resilient, scalable, and secure network infrastructures.

Chapter 4: TCP/IP Protocol Suite Essentials

In comprehending the architecture and functioning of computer networks, an essential concept to grasp is the TCP/IP protocol stack. The TCP/IP (Transmission Control Protocol/Internet Protocol) stack serves as the foundation for network communication, defining a set of protocols that facilitate data exchange and routing across interconnected networks. Each layer of the TCP/IP protocol stack performs specific functions, contributing to the end-to-end communication process and ensuring the reliable transmission of data between devices. By exploring the layers of the TCP/IP protocol stack and understanding their roles and interactions, network professionals can troubleshoot network issues, design robust network architectures, and optimize network performance.

At the core of the TCP/IP protocol stack is the Internet Protocol Suite, consisting of four main layers: the Application layer, Transport layer, Internet layer, and Link layer. Each layer addresses specific aspects of network communication, providing a hierarchical structure for organizing and managing network protocols and services.

Starting at the top of the TCP/IP protocol stack is the Application layer, which interfaces directly with end-user applications and services. The Application layer encompasses a wide range of protocols and services, including HTTP (Hypertext Transfer Protocol) for web browsing, FTP (File Transfer Protocol) for file transfer, SMTP (Simple Mail Transfer Protocol) for email transmission, and DNS (Domain Name System) for domain name resolution. Command example: "curl" to transfer data from or to a server using various protocols.

Beneath the Application layer is the Transport layer, responsible for end-to-end communication and error recovery mechanisms between host devices. The Transport layer provides two main protocols: TCP (Transmission Control Protocol) and UDP (User Datagram Protocol). TCP ensures reliable, connection-oriented data transmission by providing features such as sequencing, flow control, and error detection. UDP, on the other hand, offers connectionless, unreliable data transmission, making it suitable for applications where speed and efficiency are prioritized over reliability. Command example: "netstat" to display network statistics and active connections.

Moving down the TCP/IP protocol stack, we encounter the Internet layer, which handles logical addressing, routing, and packet forwarding across interconnected networks. The Internet layer is primarily governed by the Internet Protocol (IP), which assigns unique IP addresses to devices and enables them to communicate with each other over the internet. IP provides the framework for routing data packets between source and destination devices based on their IP addresses and network topology. Command example: "ping" to test connectivity to a remote host using ICMP (Internet Control Message Protocol).

At the bottom of the TCP/IP protocol stack is the Link layer, also known as the Network Access layer or Network Interface layer. This layer deals with the physical transmission of data over the network medium, including tasks such as data framing, error detection, and media access control. The Link layer encompasses various protocols and technologies, such as Ethernet, Wi-Fi, and PPP (Point-to-Point Protocol), which define the rules and conventions for transmitting data between network devices. Command example: "ifconfig" to display network interface configuration details.

The TCP/IP protocol stack follows a modular and hierarchical design, with each layer building upon the functionalities provided by the layer below it. This modular approach allows for flexibility, scalability, and interoperability in network communication, as different protocols and services can be added or removed without affecting the overall architecture. Additionally, the TCP/IP protocol stack adheres to the principle of encapsulation, wherein data is encapsulated into packets at each layer of the stack, with each layer adding its own header information for routing and processing purposes.

Understanding the TCP/IP protocol stack is essential for network professionals tasked with designing, deploying, and managing computer networks. By familiarizing themselves with the layers of the TCP/IP protocol stack and their respective functions, network professionals can diagnose network issues, optimize network performance, and implement effective communication protocols. As networks continue to evolve and grow in complexity, a solid understanding of the TCP/IP protocol stack remains indispensable for building resilient, scalable, and efficient network infrastructures.

In the realm of network communication, two fundamental protocols, TCP (Transmission Control Protocol) and UDP (User Datagram Protocol), play pivotal roles in facilitating data transmission across computer networks. While both TCP and UDP are part of the TCP/IP protocol suite and serve similar purposes, they exhibit distinct characteristics and are suited for different use cases. Understanding the key differences between TCP and UDP, as well as their respective strengths and weaknesses, is essential for network administrators and developers tasked with designing and managing network applications.

At the heart of the TCP vs. UDP comparison lies the manner in which each protocol handles data transmission. TCP is a connection-oriented protocol that ensures reliable and ordered delivery of data between communicating devices. It achieves reliability through features such as acknowledgment mechanisms, retransmission of lost packets, and sequencing of data segments. Command example: "netstat" to display network statistics and active connections. TCP establishes a virtual connection between sender and receiver before data exchange begins, providing guarantees for data delivery and integrity.

On the other hand, UDP is a connectionless protocol that offers minimal overhead and reduced latency compared to TCP. Unlike TCP, UDP does not establish a connection or perform reliability checks on data transmission. Instead, UDP simply encapsulates data into datagrams and sends them across the network without guaranteeing delivery or order. While UDP lacks the error recovery mechanisms of TCP, it is favored for applications where speed and efficiency are prioritized over reliability, such as real-time multimedia streaming, online gaming, and DNS (Domain Name System) resolution. Command example: "ping" to test connectivity to a remote host using ICMP (Internet Control Message Protocol).

One of the key differences between TCP and UDP lies in their approach to error handling and congestion control. TCP employs a sophisticated set of mechanisms, including flow control, congestion avoidance, and retransmission timeouts, to ensure reliable data delivery and prevent network congestion. These mechanisms enable TCP to adapt to varying network conditions and maintain optimal performance even in the presence of packet loss or network congestion. Command example: "tcptraceroute" to trace the route packets take through a TCP network.

In contrast, UDP does not incorporate error recovery or congestion control mechanisms, leaving these responsibilities to higher-layer protocols or applications. While this lack of overhead makes UDP lightweight and efficient for certain applications, it also means that UDP is more susceptible to packet loss, duplication, and out-of-order delivery. Consequently, applications built on UDP must implement their own error detection and correction mechanisms, or tolerate occasional data loss or corruption. Command example: "iperf" to measure UDP throughput between two hosts.

Another crucial difference between TCP and UDP is their suitability for different types of applications and use cases. TCP is well-suited for applications that require reliable and ordered data delivery, such as web browsing, email communication, file transfer, and database transactions. In these applications, the guaranteed delivery and integrity provided by TCP are paramount, outweighing the overhead associated with connection establishment and reliability checks. Command example: "telnet" to establish a TCP connection to a remote host.

Conversely, UDP is preferred for applications where speed, low latency, and real-time responsiveness are critical, even at the expense of occasional data loss or out-of-order delivery. Real-time multimedia streaming, VoIP (Voice over Internet Protocol), online gaming, and live video conferencing are examples of applications that benefit from UDP's lightweight and efficient data transmission model. Command example: "iperf" to measure UDP throughput between two hosts.

In summary, TCP and UDP are two fundamental protocols that serve distinct purposes in network communication. TCP provides reliable, connection-oriented communication with features such as acknowledgment, sequencing, and error recovery, making it suitable for applications that prioritize data integrity and ordered delivery. UDP, on the other hand, offers lightweight, connectionless communication with minimal overhead and reduced latency, making it ideal for real-time, latency-sensitive applications where speed and responsiveness are paramount. By understanding the key differences and use cases of TCP and UDP, network administrators and developers can make informed decisions when designing and implementing network applications.

Chapter 5: Ethernet and LAN Technologies

Ethernet, the ubiquitous networking technology, has evolved over the years, giving rise to various standards and variants that cater to different network requirements and speeds. Understanding Ethernet standards and variants is crucial for network professionals tasked with designing, implementing, and managing computer networks. Ethernet standards define the rules and specifications for transmitting data packets over Ethernet networks, while variants introduce enhancements or modifications to meet specific needs or address emerging technologies. By exploring Ethernet standards and variants, network professionals can make informed decisions when selecting networking equipment and designing network architectures.

The Institute of Electrical and Electronics Engineers (IEEE) is responsible for developing and maintaining Ethernet standards, ensuring interoperability and compatibility among networking devices from different manufacturers. One of the earliest Ethernet standards is 10BASE5, which was introduced in the 1980s and used thick coaxial cable to connect devices in a bus topology. Command example: "show interfaces" to display interface details on a Cisco switch. However, 10BASE5 was soon replaced by more advanced and flexible standards, such as 10BASE-T and 100BASE-TX.

10BASE-T and 100BASE-TX are Ethernet standards that utilize twisted pair copper cabling, enabling faster data transmission speeds and more reliable connectivity. These standards support speeds of 10 Mbps and 100 Mbps, respectively, and are widely deployed in Ethernet networks for connecting devices such as computers, printers, and switches. Command example: "ethtool" to display Ethernet adapter information on a Linux system. The adoption of twisted pair cabling made Ethernet more affordable and accessible, driving its widespread adoption in both residential and commercial environments.

As network bandwidth requirements continued to increase, the IEEE introduced Gigabit Ethernet (GbE) standards to support data rates of 1 gigabit per second (Gbps) over twisted pair copper cabling. The most commonly deployed Gigabit Ethernet standard is 1000BASE-T, which operates at a speed of 1 Gbps over Cat 5e or higher-grade twisted pair cables. Command example: "ifconfig" to display network interface configuration details on a Unix-based system. 1000BASE-T offers significant performance improvements over previous Ethernet standards and is widely used in modern LANs and data center networks.

To meet the demands of high-performance computing and data-intensive applications, the IEEE developed 10 Gigabit Ethernet (10GbE) standards, which support data rates of 10 Gbps over various media types, including copper and fiber optic cables. 10GBASE-T is a 10GbE standard that utilizes twisted pair copper cabling for connectivity, offering cost-effective and scalable solutions for high-speed network deployments. Command example: "ethtool -S" to display Ethernet adapter statistics on a Linux system. 10GBASE-T is commonly used in enterprise networks, cloud environments, and storage area networks (SANs).

In addition to copper-based Ethernet standards, fiber optic Ethernet variants have gained popularity for their higher data rates, longer transmission distances, and immunity to electromagnetic interference. Ethernet over Fiber standards, such as 1000BASE-SX and 1000BASE-LX, utilize multimode and single-mode fiber optic cables, respectively, to support gigabit data rates over extended distances. Command example: "show interface transceiver" to display optical transceiver details on a Cisco switch. These standards are commonly deployed in enterprise networks, campus networks, and metropolitan area networks (MANs).

To keep pace with evolving networking technologies and address the demand for even higher data rates, the IEEE has developed advanced Ethernet standards such as 25 Gigabit Ethernet (25GbE), 40 Gigabit Ethernet (40GbE), and 100 Gigabit Ethernet (100GbE). These standards support data rates of 25 Gbps, 40 Gbps, and 100 Gbps, respectively, catering to the needs of modern data center networks and high-performance computing environments. Command example: "show interface status" to display interface status on a Cisco device. These high-speed Ethernet standards utilize a combination of fiber optic and copper cabling technologies to deliver fast and reliable connectivity.

In summary, Ethernet standards and variants play a critical role in defining the capabilities and performance of Ethernet networks. From the early days of 10BASE-T to the latest advancements in 100GbE and beyond, Ethernet continues to evolve to meet the growing demands of modern networking environments. By understanding the characteristics and applications of different Ethernet standards and variants, network professionals can design scalable, high-performance networks that meet the requirements of today's digital age.

Setting up and configuring a Local Area Network (LAN) is a fundamental task for network administrators and IT professionals responsible for managing organizational networks. A well-designed and properly configured LAN is essential for ensuring efficient communication, reliable connectivity, and secure data transmission within an organization's premises. LAN setup and configuration involve various steps and considerations, including network design, hardware selection, IP addressing, subnetting, VLAN configuration, and security implementation. By following established guidelines and best practices, network administrators can deploy robust LAN infrastructures that meet the needs of their organizations.

The first step in LAN setup and configuration is to plan the network design and layout. This involves assessing the organization's requirements, identifying network segments or departments, and determining the physical and logical topology of the LAN. Common network topologies include star, bus, ring, and mesh, with the star topology being the most widely used in LAN environments. Command example: "ipconfig /all" to display IP configuration details on a Windows system.

Once the network design is finalized, network administrators can proceed with selecting the appropriate networking hardware.

Hardware selection is a critical aspect of LAN setup and configuration, as it determines the performance, scalability, and reliability of the network infrastructure. Key hardware components include switches, routers, access points, network interface cards (NICs), and cabling. When selecting switches and routers, factors such as port density, throughput, and support for advanced features like VLANs and Quality of Service (QoS) should be considered. Command example: "show version" to display hardware and software information on a Cisco device. For wireless LANs, access points should be strategically placed to provide optimal coverage and minimize interference.

IP addressing and subnetting are essential tasks in LAN setup and configuration, as they enable devices to communicate and route data within the network. Administrators must assign unique IP addresses to devices within the LAN and organize them into logical subnets to optimize network traffic and facilitate routing. IP addressing schemes should adhere to the organization's addressing plan and consider factors such as scalability and ease of management. Command example: "ifconfig" to display network interface configuration details on a Unix-based system. Subnetting can be performed using tools like subnet calculators or by manually dividing IP address ranges into subnets based on network requirements.

VLAN (Virtual Local Area Network) configuration is another important aspect of LAN setup and configuration, particularly in large or complex network environments. VLANs enable administrators to logically segment the LAN into multiple broadcast domains, improving network performance, security, and management. VLAN configuration involves assigning ports on switches to specific VLANs, configuring VLAN interfaces on routers, and implementing VLAN trunking protocols to carry VLAN traffic between switches. Command example: "show vlan" to display VLAN information on a Cisco switch. VLANs should be designed based on departmental boundaries, security requirements, and traffic patterns.

Security implementation is a critical consideration in LAN setup and configuration to protect against unauthorized access, data breaches, and network threats. Security measures may include implementing access control lists (ACLs), enabling port security, deploying intrusion detection and prevention systems (IDPS), and configuring firewalls and VPNs (Virtual Private Networks) to secure remote access. Command example: "show access-list" to display access control list entries on a Cisco router. Additionally, administrators should regularly update firmware and software patches to mitigate security vulnerabilities and ensure the integrity of the LAN infrastructure.

Monitoring and management are ongoing tasks in LAN setup and configuration to ensure the smooth operation and performance of the network. Network monitoring tools can be used to monitor traffic, detect network issues, and troubleshoot connectivity problems. Command example: "netstat" to display network statistics and active connections. Network management protocols such as SNMP (Simple Network Management Protocol) allow administrators to centrally manage and configure network devices, collect performance data, and generate reports for analysis.

In summary, LAN setup and configuration involves a series of steps and considerations aimed at designing, deploying, and managing a robust and secure LAN infrastructure. By following established guidelines and best practices, network administrators can create LANs that meet the needs of their organizations in terms of performance, scalability, reliability, and security. Regular monitoring, maintenance, and updates are essential to ensure the ongoing operation and optimization of the LAN infrastructure. With careful planning and attention to detail, LAN setup and configuration can lay the foundation for a resilient and efficient network environment.

Chapter 6: Wireless Networking Fundamentals

Wireless communication has revolutionized the way we connect and interact with technology, enabling mobility, flexibility, and convenience in various applications and industries. A multitude of wireless communication standards have emerged over the years, each designed to meet specific requirements, address different use cases, and optimize performance in wireless networks. Understanding these wireless communication standards is essential for network engineers, system integrators, and technology enthusiasts seeking to deploy, manage, and optimize wireless networks effectively. From Wi-Fi to Bluetooth, Zigbee, LTE, and 5G, these standards play a crucial role in shaping the future of wireless connectivity.

Wi-Fi, perhaps the most ubiquitous wireless communication standard, provides wireless LAN connectivity using radio waves. The IEEE 802.11 family of standards governs Wi-Fi technology, with variations such as 802.11b/g/n/ac/ax offering different speeds, frequency bands, and features. Command example: "iwconfig" to display wireless interface configuration on a Linux system. Wi-Fi standards operate in the 2.4 GHz and 5 GHz frequency bands and support data rates ranging from a few megabits per second to several gigabits per second, catering to a wide range of applications from home networking to enterprise deployments.

Bluetooth is another widely adopted wireless communication standard designed for short-range communication between devices. The Bluetooth Special Interest Group (SIG) develops and maintains the Bluetooth standard, with versions like Bluetooth 4.0, 5.0, and Bluetooth Low Energy (BLE) offering enhanced features such as improved range, data rates, and power efficiency. Command example: "bluetoothctl" to manage Bluetooth devices on a Linux system. Bluetooth technology is commonly used for wireless audio streaming, file transfer, device pairing, and IoT (Internet of Things) applications.

Zigbee is a low-power, low-data-rate wireless communication standard optimized for IoT and home automation applications. The Zigbee Alliance develops and promotes the Zigbee standard, which operates in the 2.4 GHz frequency band and offers mesh networking capabilities, allowing devices to communicate over extended distances. Command example: "zigbee-herdsman" to manage Zigbee devices in a home automation system. Zigbee technology is commonly used in smart home devices, industrial automation, smart lighting, and environmental monitoring applications.

Long-Term Evolution (LTE) is a wireless communication standard developed for high-speed mobile broadband access. LTE, also known as 4G LTE, provides faster data rates, lower latency, and improved spectral efficiency compared to previous cellular technologies. Command example: "lte-status" to display LTE modem status on a Linux system. LTE technology is widely deployed by mobile operators worldwide to deliver mobile internet access, video streaming, VoIP (Voice over Internet Protocol), and other data-intensive services to smartphones, tablets, and IoT devices.

5G, the latest generation of wireless communication technology, promises even higher data rates, lower latency, and greater network capacity compared to 4G LTE. The 3rd Generation Partnership Project (3GPP) develops and standardizes 5G technology, which operates in both sub-6 GHz and mmWave frequency bands. Command example: "show 5g-info" to display 5G network information on a mobile device. 5G technology enables new applications such as augmented reality, virtual reality, autonomous vehicles, and massive IoT deployments, transforming industries and driving innovation in wireless communication.

Other wireless communication standards include NFC (Near Field Communication), RFID (Radio Frequency Identification), LoRaWAN (Long Range Wide Area Network), and satellite communication systems. NFC enables short-range communication between devices for contactless payments, ticketing, and data transfer. Command example: "nfc-list" to list NFC devices on a Linux system. RFID technology is used for asset tracking, inventory management, access control, and identification purposes in various industries. Command example: "rfidreader" to read RFID tags on a Raspberry Pi device.

LoRaWAN is a low-power, wide-area wireless communication standard designed for long-range IoT applications such as smart agriculture, smart cities, and environmental monitoring. Command example: "lorawanctl" to manage LoRaWAN devices and gateways. Satellite communication systems provide global coverage for voice, data, and multimedia services, enabling connectivity in remote and rural areas where terrestrial infrastructure is limited or unavailable. Command example: "satcom-status" to display satellite communication status on a satellite modem.

In summary, wireless communication standards play a vital role in enabling connectivity, mobility, and innovation in modern society. From Wi-Fi and Bluetooth to Zigbee, LTE, 5G, and beyond, these standards provide the foundation for a wide range of wireless applications and services. By understanding the characteristics, features, and deployment scenarios of different wireless communication standards, technology professionals can design, deploy, and manage wireless networks that meet the diverse needs of users and industries. As wireless technology continues to evolve, new standards and advancements will shape the future of wireless communication, driving connectivity and innovation worldwide.

Securing wireless networks is paramount in today's digital landscape, where the proliferation of wireless devices and the increasing sophistication of cyber threats pose significant challenges to network security. Implementing robust security measures is essential to protect sensitive data, prevent unauthorized access, and safeguard the integrity of wireless communications. By following best practices and adopting industry-standard security protocols, organizations can mitigate risks and ensure the confidentiality, integrity, and availability of their wireless networks.

One of the first steps in securing a wireless network is to change the default administrative credentials of network devices such as wireless routers, access points, and switches. Default credentials are often well-known and easily exploitable by attackers, making it crucial to set strong, unique passwords for device administration. Command example: "enable secret" to set an encrypted enable password on a Cisco device. Additionally, administrators should disable any unnecessary services or features that could serve as potential attack vectors.

Implementing strong encryption protocols is essential to protect wireless communications from eavesdropping and unauthorized interception. Wi-Fi Protected Access (WPA) and WPA2 are widely used encryption standards that provide robust security for wireless networks. Command example: "wpa_supplicant" to configure WPA or WPA2 encryption on a Linux system. WPA3, the latest iteration of the WPA standard, offers enhanced security features such as stronger encryption algorithms and protection against brute-force attacks, providing an additional layer of defense against wireless threats.

Enabling Wi-Fi Protected Access Pre-Shared Key (WPA-PSK) or Wi-Fi Protected Access Enterprise (WPA-EAP) authentication mechanisms adds an extra layer of security to wireless networks by requiring users to authenticate themselves before gaining access. WPA-PSK uses a pre-shared passphrase or key for authentication, while WPA-EAP leverages an external authentication server such as RADIUS (Remote

Authentication Dial-In User Service) for user authentication. Command example: "wpa_supplicant -B -i wlan0 -c /etc/wpa_supplicant.conf -Dwext" to start WPA authentication on a Linux system.

Implementing MAC address filtering is another effective security measure to control access to wireless networks. MAC address filtering allows administrators to specify which devices are allowed or denied access based on their MAC (Media Access Control) addresses. While MAC address filtering alone is not foolproof, it adds an additional layer of defense against unauthorized devices attempting to connect to the network. Command example: "mac access-list extended" to configure MAC address filtering on a Cisco router or switch.

Regularly updating firmware and software patches is essential to address known security vulnerabilities and protect against emerging threats in wireless networking equipment and devices. Manufacturers release firmware updates and security patches to address vulnerabilities and improve the security posture of their products. Command example: "show version" to display firmware and software information on a network device. Administrators should monitor vendor websites and subscribe to security advisories to stay informed about the latest updates.

Securing the physical environment of wireless network infrastructure is critical to prevent unauthorized access and tampering. Access points and wireless routers should be installed in secure locations inaccessible to unauthorized individuals. Additionally, physical security measures such as locks, surveillance cameras, and access control systems can deter unauthorized access to network equipment and prevent physical attacks on wireless networks.

Implementing intrusion detection and prevention systems (IDPS) and network monitoring tools allows administrators to detect and respond to security threats in real-time. IDPS solutions monitor network traffic for suspicious activity, such as unauthorized access attempts, malware infections, and denial-of-service attacks, and take automated actions to block or mitigate threats. Command example: "show ip inspect" to display IP inspection configuration on a Cisco router.

Enforcing strong password policies and user authentication mechanisms is crucial to prevent unauthorized access to wireless networks. Passwords should be complex, unique, and regularly rotated to reduce the risk of brute-force attacks and password guessing. Multi-factor authentication (MFA) provides an additional layer of security by requiring users to authenticate themselves using multiple factors such as passwords, security tokens, or biometric credentials. Command example: "username" to configure user authentication on a Cisco device.

Implementing network segmentation and isolation is a best practice to limit the impact of security breaches and contain potential threats within specific network segments. By segmenting the network into separate VLANs (Virtual Local Area Networks) and implementing access control policies, administrators can control traffic flows, enforce security policies, and minimize the attack surface of wireless networks. Command example: "vlan" to configure VLANs on a Cisco switch.

Regular security audits and vulnerability assessments are essential to identify and address security weaknesses in wireless networks. Security audits involve reviewing network configurations, access controls, and security policies to ensure compliance with industry standards and best practices. Vulnerability assessments use automated tools and manual techniques to identify security vulnerabilities and assess the effectiveness of security controls in protecting wireless networks. Command example: "show security" to display security configuration details on a network device.

Chapter 7: Internet and Intranet Concepts

Understanding the distinction between the Internet and an intranet is fundamental in today's interconnected digital landscape. While both concepts involve networks and data exchange, they serve distinct purposes and cater to different audiences. The Internet, often referred to as the "World Wide Web," is a global network of interconnected computers and devices that allows users to access and share information across geographic boundaries. Command example: "ping www.example.com" to test connectivity to a website. In contrast, an intranet is a private network restricted to an organization or group of users, providing internal communication, collaboration, and information sharing capabilities.

The Internet, as a vast and decentralized network, facilitates communication and data exchange between millions of devices worldwide. It operates on a global scale, connecting individuals, businesses, governments, and organizations across continents and time zones. The Internet relies on standard protocols such as TCP/IP (Transmission Control Protocol/Internet Protocol) to enable seamless communication between devices regardless of their location or underlying technology. Command example: "traceroute" to trace the route packets take across the Internet to reach a destination.

One of the defining features of the Internet is its openness and accessibility, allowing users to access a wealth of information and services hosted on remote servers. Websites, web applications, email services, social media platforms, and cloud-based services are among the myriad resources available on the Internet. Users can access these resources using web browsers, email clients, and other Internet-enabled applications from virtually any location with an Internet connection. Command example: "telnet" to establish a TCP connection to a remote server over the Internet.

The Internet also serves as a platform for e-commerce, online banking, digital entertainment, and communication services, enabling businesses and individuals to conduct transactions, share content, and collaborate in real-time. Online shopping websites, banking portals, streaming platforms, and messaging apps are examples of Internet-based services that have become integral parts of modern life. Command example: "curl" to transfer data from or to a server using various protocols such as HTTP, HTTPS, FTP, etc.

In contrast to the Internet's global reach and public accessibility, an intranet is a private network confined within the boundaries of an organization or enterprise. Command example: "ipconfig" to display IP configuration details on a Windows system connected to an intranet. Intranets are used to facilitate internal communication, collaboration, and information sharing among employees, departments, and stakeholders. They typically utilize standard networking technologies such as Ethernet, Wi-Fi, and TCP/IP but operate within a restricted environment controlled by the organization.

One of the primary purposes of an intranet is to provide employees with access to corporate resources, documents, databases, and applications essential for their work. Intranets often feature centralized repositories such as document libraries, knowledge bases, and employee directories, allowing users to find and retrieve information quickly and efficiently. Command example: "net use" to map a network drive to a shared folder on an intranet server. Intranets also support internal communication tools such as email, instant messaging, and video conferencing for collaboration and teamwork.

Security is a critical concern in both Internet and intranet environments, but the focus and approach differ significantly. While the Internet is inherently more exposed to external threats such as cyberattacks, malware, and data breaches, intranets are typically shielded from external access by firewalls, access controls, and other security measures. Command example: "iptables" to configure firewall rules on a Linux server protecting an intranet. Intranets also employ encryption, authentication, and authorization mechanisms to ensure the confidentiality and integrity of sensitive information.

Another key difference between the Internet and intranet is their scope and audience. The Internet caters to a diverse global audience, including individuals, businesses, governments, and organizations, with no geographical or organizational boundaries. In contrast, an intranet serves a specific organization or group of users, providing tailored content and services relevant to their needs and roles within the organization.

Command example: "groupadd" to create a new user group on an intranet server.

In summary, the Internet and intranet are distinct concepts with unique characteristics, purposes, and audiences. The Internet is a global network of interconnected computers and devices that facilitates communication, collaboration, and information sharing on a global scale. In contrast, an intranet is a private network restricted to an organization or group of users, providing internal communication, collaboration, and access to corporate resources. Understanding the differences between the Internet and intranet is essential for effectively leveraging these networks to meet the diverse needs of users and organizations in the digital age.

The Internet is a vast and complex network comprising various interconnected components that work together to facilitate communication, data exchange, and information dissemination on a global scale. Understanding the infrastructure components of the Internet is crucial for network engineers, system administrators, and technology enthusiasts seeking to grasp the underlying architecture and functionality of this ubiquitous network. From physical infrastructure such as cables and routers to logical components like domain names and protocols, each element plays a vital role in the seamless operation of the Internet.

Physical infrastructure forms the backbone of the Internet, consisting of cables, fiber-optic lines, switches, routers, and data centers that transmit and route data across vast distances. Undersea cables, also known as submarine communications cables, are essential components of the Internet's physical infrastructure, carrying vast amounts of data between continents. Command example: "traceroute" to trace the path data packets take through routers and switches on the Internet. These cables connect countries and continents, forming the foundation of global connectivity.

Fiber-optic lines are another critical component of the Internet's physical infrastructure, providing high-speed data transmission over long distances. Fiber-optic cables use light signals to transmit data, offering greater bandwidth and faster speeds compared to traditional copper cables. Command example: "ifconfig" to display network interface configuration details, including information about fiber-optic connections. These cables are used by telecommunications companies and Internet service providers (ISPs) to build high-capacity networks that span continents and regions.

Switches and routers play a crucial role in routing and forwarding data across the Internet's physical infrastructure. Switches are responsible for connecting devices within local networks and forwarding data packets to their intended destinations. Routers, on the other hand, are responsible for directing data between different networks, determining the optimal path for data transmission based on routing protocols such as OSPF (Open Shortest Path First) and BGP (Border Gateway Protocol). Command example: "show ip route" to display the routing table on a router. Together, switches and routers form the backbone of the Internet, enabling data to flow between networks seamlessly.

Data centers are centralized facilities that house servers, storage devices, networking equipment, and other hardware essential for hosting websites, web applications, and online services. Command example: "ls" to list files and directories on a Linux server hosted in a data center. These facilities provide the computing power and storage capacity needed to support the vast array of online content and services available on the Internet. Data centers are strategically located near major Internet exchange points (IXPs) to minimize latency and ensure reliable connectivity.

Domain names and IP addresses are fundamental components of the Internet's addressing system, allowing users to access websites and online services using human-readable names instead of numerical IP addresses. Domain names, such as example.com or google.com, provide a memorable and intuitive way to identify websites and resources on the Internet. Command example: "nslookup" to query DNS (Domain Name System) servers and resolve domain names to IP addresses. DNS translates domain names into IP addresses, enabling computers and devices to locate and connect to websites and services.

Protocols are standardized rules and procedures that govern communication and data exchange on the Internet. TCP/IP (Transmission Control Protocol/Internet Protocol) is the foundational protocol suite of the Internet, defining how data is transmitted, routed, and received between devices on the network.

Command example: "tcpdump" to capture and analyze network traffic using TCP/IP protocols. TCP/IP comprises several layers, including the application layer, transport layer, network layer, and link layer, each responsible for specific aspects of data communication and networking. HTTP (Hypertext Transfer Protocol) and HTTPS (HTTP Secure) are application-layer protocols used for transferring web pages, images, and other content over the Internet. Command example: "curl" to transfer data from or to a web server using HTTP or HTTPS protocols. HTTPS adds an extra layer of security by encrypting data transmitted between web browsers and servers, protecting it from interception and tampering by malicious actors. These protocols are fundamental to accessing and interacting with websites and web services on the Internet.

SMTP (Simple Mail Transfer Protocol) and IMAP (Internet Message Access Protocol) are protocols used for sending and receiving email messages over the Internet. Command example: "telnet" to establish a connection to an email server using SMTP. SMTP is responsible for sending outgoing email messages, while IMAP enables users to access and manage their email messages stored on a remote server. These protocols enable efficient and reliable email communication, facilitating correspondence between individuals and organizations worldwide.

DNS (Domain Name System) is a distributed system that translates domain names into IP addresses, allowing computers and devices to locate and connect to websites and services on the Internet. Command example: "dig" to perform DNS queries and retrieve information about domain names, IP addresses, and DNS records. DNS operates using a hierarchical structure of DNS servers, including root servers, top-level domain (TLD) servers, authoritative name servers, and recursive resolvers, to efficiently resolve domain names to IP addresses.

Firewalls and security appliances are essential components of Internet infrastructure, providing protection against unauthorized access, malicious attacks, and data breaches. Firewalls monitor and control incoming and outgoing network traffic based on predefined security rules, preventing unauthorized access to network resources and blocking malicious traffic. Command example: "iptables" to configure firewall rules on a Linux server protecting a network. Security appliances such as intrusion detection systems (IDS) and intrusion prevention systems (IPS) detect and respond to security threats in real-time, enhancing the overall security posture of Internet-connected networks.

In summary, the Internet's infrastructure comprises a diverse array of physical and logical components that work together to facilitate global communication, data exchange, and information dissemination. From cables and routers to protocols and security mechanisms, each component plays a crucial role in ensuring the reliability, security, and functionality of the Internet. Understanding these components is essential for effectively managing and optimizing Internet-connected networks and services in today's digital age.

Chapter 8: Network Devices and Infrastructure

Routers, switches, and hubs are fundamental networking devices that play distinct roles in the operation and management of computer networks. Each device serves specific functions and performs essential tasks to facilitate communication, data transmission, and network connectivity. Understanding the functions of routers, switches, and hubs is essential for network administrators, engineers, and enthusiasts seeking to design, configure, and optimize network infrastructures for optimal performance and reliability.

Routers are critical networking devices that operate at the network layer (Layer 3) of the OSI model and are responsible for forwarding data packets between different networks. Routers use routing tables and algorithms to determine the optimal path for data transmission based on destination IP addresses. Command example: "show ip route" to display the routing table on a router. By examining the destination IP address of incoming packets, routers determine the next hop or interface through which the packets should be forwarded, ensuring efficient and reliable data delivery across complex network topologies.

One of the primary functions of routers is to interconnect multiple networks, enabling devices on different networks to communicate with each other. Routers establish logical network boundaries, segregating traffic and preventing broadcast storms and network congestion. Command example: "ip route" to configure static or dynamic routing on a router. By maintaining routing tables and exchanging routing information with neighboring routers using routing protocols such as OSPF (Open Shortest Path First) and BGP (Border Gateway Protocol), routers ensure seamless communication between disparate network segments.

Routers also provide network address translation (NAT) and firewall functionality to secure and manage network traffic. NAT allows multiple devices on a private network to share a single public IP address when accessing the Internet, conserving public IP addresses and providing an additional layer of security by hiding internal IP addresses from external networks. Command example: "ip nat inside source" to configure NAT on a router. Firewalls implemented on routers filter incoming and outgoing traffic based on predefined security policies, protecting network resources from unauthorized access and malicious attacks.

Switches are essential networking devices that operate at the data link layer (Layer 2) of the OSI model and are responsible for connecting devices within the same network segment or LAN (Local Area Network). Switches use MAC (Media Access Control) addresses to forward data packets to their intended destinations within the same network. Command example: "show mac address-table" to display the MAC address table on a switch. By examining the destination MAC address of incoming frames, switches forward frames only to the appropriate ports, preventing unnecessary broadcast and multicast traffic.

One of the primary functions of switches is to provide high-speed, low-latency connectivity between devices within the same network segment. Switches use hardware-based switching mechanisms to forward data packets at wire speed, ensuring fast and efficient communication between connected devices. Command example: "interface range" to configure multiple interfaces on a switch. Switches also support VLAN (Virtual Local Area Network) technology, allowing network administrators to logically segment network traffic and control broadcast domains within a single physical network infrastructure.

Switches facilitate full-duplex communication, allowing devices to transmit and receive data simultaneously on separate communication channels. Unlike hubs, which operate at the physical layer (Layer 1) of the OSI model and share bandwidth among connected devices, switches provide dedicated bandwidth to each connected device, minimizing collisions and maximizing network performance. Command example: "speed" and "duplex" to configure interface speed and duplex mode on a switch. By dynamically learning MAC addresses and populating MAC address tables, switches ensure efficient frame forwarding and optimal network throughput.

Hubs, although less commonly used in modern networks, are simple networking devices that operate at the physical layer (Layer 1) of the OSI model and function as multi-port repeaters. Hubs receive incoming data packets on one port and broadcast them to all other ports, regardless of the destination MAC address, effectively duplicating the traffic across all connected devices. Command example: N/A - hubs are plug-and-play devices with no configuration options. Unlike switches, hubs do not perform any packet filtering or forwarding based on MAC addresses, making them less efficient in managing network traffic and bandwidth utilization.

One of the primary functions of hubs is to provide a centralized connection point for devices within the same network segment, allowing them to communicate with each other using shared bandwidth. However, due to their limited intelligence and lack of packet filtering capabilities, hubs are prone to network congestion, collisions, and performance degradation, especially in larger network environments. Command example: N/A - hubs do not have configuration options or CLI interfaces. In modern network deployments, switches have largely replaced hubs due to their superior performance, scalability, and manageability.

In summary, routers, switches, and hubs are essential networking devices that perform distinct functions in computer networks. Routers interconnect multiple networks, forward data packets between networks, and provide network addressing and security services. Switches connect devices within the same network segment, facilitate high-speed communication, and optimize network performance. Hubs provide basic connectivity and broadcast incoming data packets to all connected devices within the same network segment. Understanding the functions and capabilities of routers, switches, and hubs is essential for designing, configuring, and managing efficient and reliable network infrastructures.

Designing a robust and efficient network infrastructure requires careful planning, analysis, and consideration of various factors to meet the diverse needs and requirements of organizations. Command example: "show interface status" to display the status of interfaces on network devices. From network topology and scalability to security and performance, network administrators and architects must evaluate multiple aspects to create a network infrastructure that is scalable, resilient, and capable of supporting current and future business objectives.

One of the first considerations in network infrastructure design is determining the appropriate network topology based on organizational requirements and objectives. Command example: "show cdp neighbors" to display CDP (Cisco Discovery Protocol) neighbors on a Cisco router or switch. Common network topologies include star, mesh, ring, and hybrid topologies, each offering unique advantages and disadvantages in terms of scalability, fault tolerance, and ease of management. By selecting the right topology, organizations can optimize network performance, minimize downtime, and improve overall efficiency.

Scalability is another critical aspect of network infrastructure design, especially for organizations experiencing growth or expansion. Command example: "show ip bgp summary" to display BGP (Border Gateway Protocol) summary information on a router. Network architects must design a scalable infrastructure that can accommodate future growth in terms of network traffic, devices, and users without compromising performance or reliability. This may involve deploying redundant links, implementing VLANs (Virtual Local Area Networks), and using routing protocols that support dynamic routing and load balancing.

Security is paramount in network infrastructure design, particularly with the increasing prevalence of cyber threats and attacks. Command example: "show access-list" to display access control lists (ACLs) configured on a router or switch. Organizations must implement robust security measures to protect sensitive data, prevent unauthorized access, and mitigate security risks. This may include deploying firewalls, intrusion detection and prevention systems (IDPS), VPNs (Virtual Private Networks), and access control mechanisms to enforce security policies and safeguard network resources.

Performance optimization is a key consideration in network infrastructure design to ensure that the network meets the demands of users and applications. Command example: "show interface gigabitethernet" to display detailed interface statistics on a switch or router. Network architects must analyze traffic patterns, identify potential bottlenecks, and optimize network performance by implementing Quality of Service (QoS) policies, traffic shaping, and bandwidth management techniques. This helps prioritize critical traffic, minimize latency, and ensure a consistent user experience across the network.

Reliability and resilience are essential aspects of network infrastructure design to minimize downtime and ensure continuous operation of critical business processes. Command example: "show spanning-tree" to display Spanning Tree Protocol (STP) information on a switch. Redundancy and fault tolerance mechanisms such as link aggregation, redundant links, and failover configurations help improve network resilience and mitigate the impact of network failures or hardware malfunctions. By implementing redundant components and designing for high availability, organizations can minimize disruptions and maintain business continuity.

Ease of management and maintenance is crucial in network infrastructure design to simplify operations, reduce administrative overhead, and improve troubleshooting efficiency. Command example: "show running-config" to display the current configuration of a network device. Network architects should design a network infrastructure that is easy to monitor, manage, and maintain by using centralized management tools, automation solutions, and standardized configurations. This streamlines routine tasks, facilitates troubleshooting, and enhances overall network agility and responsiveness.

Integration with existing systems and technologies is an important consideration in network infrastructure design, especially in environments with legacy systems or heterogeneous architectures. Command example: "show version" to display hardware and software version information on a network device. Network architects must ensure compatibility and interoperability between new and existing network components, applications, and services to facilitate seamless integration and migration. This may involve conducting compatibility tests, implementing protocols and standards, and adopting modular or scalable solutions.

Compliance with industry standards and regulations is a critical aspect of network infrastructure design to ensure regulatory compliance, data protection, and adherence to best practices. Command example: "show ip route" to display routing information on a router. Organizations must design and configure their network infrastructure in accordance with industry standards such as TCP/IP, IEEE, and ITU-T recommendations, as well as regulatory requirements such as GDPR (General Data Protection Regulation) and HIPAA (Health Insurance Portability and Accountability Act). This helps mitigate legal and regulatory risks and demonstrates a commitment to data security and privacy.

In summary, network infrastructure design is a complex and multifaceted process that requires careful consideration of various factors, including topology, scalability, security, performance, reliability, management, integration, and compliance. By addressing these considerations comprehensively, organizations can design a robust and resilient network infrastructure that meets their current and future business needs while ensuring the security, efficiency, and reliability of their network operations.

Chapter 9: IP Addressing and Subnetting

Understanding IP address classes and addressing schemes is fundamental to designing and managing computer networks. Command example: "ip address" to configure IP addresses on network interfaces. IP addresses serve as unique identifiers for devices on a network, facilitating communication and data exchange between them. The Internet Protocol (IP) uses a hierarchical addressing structure, which divides IP addresses into classes based on the network portion and host portion of the address. This classification system, defined in RFC 791, establishes five classes of IP addresses: A, B, C, D, and E, each with specific characteristics and address ranges.

Class A addresses are designed for large networks and use the first octet to represent the network portion of the address. Command example: "ip address 10.0.0.1 255.0.0.0" to assign a Class A address to a network interface. Class A addresses can accommodate up to 16 million hosts on a single network and are identified by a leading bit pattern of "0" in the first octet. This allows for a vast number of available IP addresses, making Class A addresses suitable for large enterprises and Internet Service Providers (ISPs) that require a significant number of host addresses.

Class B addresses are intended for medium-sized networks and use the first two octets to represent the network portion of the address. Command example: "ip address 172.16.0.1 255.255.0.0" to assign a Class B address to a network interface. Class B addresses can support up to 65,534 hosts on a single network and are identified by a leading bit pattern of "10" in the first octet. This provides a balance between the scalability of Class A addresses and the efficient use of address space, making Class B addresses suitable for mid-sized organizations and educational institutions.

Class C addresses are designed for small networks and use the first three octets to represent the network portion of the address. Command example: "ip address 192.168.0.1 255.255.255.0" to assign a Class C address to a network interface. Class C addresses can accommodate up to 254 hosts on a single network and are identified by a leading bit pattern of "110" in the first octet. While Class C addresses offer limited address space compared to Class A and B addresses, they are more efficient in terms of address allocation and are commonly used in small businesses and home networks.

Class D addresses are reserved for multicast addresses and are used to deliver data to multiple recipients simultaneously. Command example: N/A - multicast addresses are not assigned to individual devices like unicast addresses. Instead, multicast addresses are used by applications and network protocols to transmit data packets to multiple recipients who have joined a specific multicast group. Class D addresses range from 224.0.0.0 to 239.255.255.255 and are identified by a leading bit pattern of "1110" in the first octet.

Class E addresses are reserved for experimental and research purposes and are not intended for general use in networking. Command example: N/A - Class E addresses are not assigned to devices or networks and are designated for future use or experimentation. Class E addresses range from 240.0.0.0 to 255.255.255.254 and are identified by a leading bit pattern of "1111" in the first octet. These addresses are reserved by the Internet Assigned Numbers Authority (IANA) for future specifications or experimental purposes.

In addition to IP address classes, various addressing schemes are used to efficiently allocate and manage IP addresses within a network. Command example: "ip address dhcp" to configure dynamic IP addressing using DHCP (Dynamic Host Configuration Protocol). Dynamic addressing schemes, such as DHCP, automatically assign IP addresses to devices on a network from a predefined pool of addresses, eliminating the need for manual configuration and simplifying network administration. Command example: "ip address 192.168.1.1 255.255.255.0" to configure static IP addressing manually. Static addressing schemes involve manually assigning IP addresses to devices, which provides greater control over network configuration but requires careful planning and management to avoid address conflicts and ensure proper addressing.

Subnetting is another addressing scheme used to divide a large network into smaller, more manageable subnetworks. Command example: "ip subnet-zero" to enable subnetting on a router. Subnetting allows organizations to optimize network performance, improve security, and conserve address space by segmenting networks into smaller, logical units called subnets. This enables more efficient use of IP addresses and simplifies network management and troubleshooting. Command example: "ip address 192.168.1.1 255.255.255.240" to assign a subnetted IP address to a network interface.

CIDR (Classless Inter-Domain Routing) is a flexible addressing scheme that allows for variable-length subnet masking and more efficient allocation of IP addresses. Command example: "ip address 192.168.1.1/24" to specify a CIDR notation for an IP address with a subnet mask of /24. CIDR enables the aggregation of IP addresses into larger blocks, reducing routing table size and improving network scalability and efficiency. By using CIDR notation, network administrators can easily represent IP address ranges and subnet masks in a concise and standardized format.

In summary, understanding IP address classes and addressing schemes is essential for designing, configuring, and managing IP networks. By leveraging the hierarchical structure of IP address classes and implementing appropriate addressing schemes such as dynamic addressing, static addressing, subnetting, and CIDR, organizations can optimize network performance, improve scalability, conserve address space, and simplify network administration. Command example: "ip address" to verify the IP address configuration on network devices.

Subnetting is a crucial networking concept that involves dividing a single large network into smaller, more manageable subnetworks. Command example: "ip subnet-zero" to enable subnetting on a router. By subnetting a network, organizations can improve network performance, enhance security, and optimize resource utilization. Subnetting requires careful planning and calculation to determine the appropriate subnet masks, subnet addresses, and host ranges for each subnet.

One of the primary benefits of subnetting is the ability to conserve IP address space by allocating addresses more efficiently. Command example: "ip address 192.168.1.1 255.255.255.0" to configure a subnetted IP address with a custom subnet mask. Instead of assigning a single large address block to a network, subnetting allows organizations to divide the address space into smaller blocks, each serving a specific subnet. This reduces wastage of IP addresses and ensures optimal utilization of available address space.

When subnetting a network, the first step is to determine the subnet mask, which defines the boundary between the network portion and the host portion of an IP address. Command example: "show ip interface brief" to display the configured IP addresses and subnet masks on network interfaces. The subnet mask is represented in binary notation as a series of consecutive ones followed by zeros, where each one corresponds to a network bit and each zero corresponds to a host bit.

To calculate the number of subnets and hosts per subnet, subnetting requires converting the subnet mask into binary form and determining the number of subnet bits and host bits. Command example: "ip address 192.168.1.0 255.255.255.128" to configure a subnet with a subnet mask of /25, allowing for 126 hosts per subnet. The number of subnet bits determines the number of subnets, while the number of host bits determines the number of hosts per subnet.

To perform subnetting calculations manually, one can use the subnetting chart or the subnetting formula. Command example: N/A - manual subnetting calculations involve converting subnet masks to binary, determining the number of subnet bits and host bits, and calculating the number of subnets and hosts per subnet using the subnetting formula.

For example, with a subnet mask of /27 (or 255.255.255.224 in decimal), there are 5 subnet bits, so the formula becomes:

$2^5-2=32-2=3025-2=32-2=30$

This means there are 30 subnets and $2^5-2=25-2$ hosts per subnet.

In addition to manual calculations, subnetting can also be performed using subnet calculators or online subnetting tools. Command example: N/A - subnet calculators are software tools that automate the subnetting process, allowing users to input the network address and desired number of subnets or hosts per subnet to generate the appropriate subnet masks and subnet addresses.

When subnetting a network, it's essential to consider factors such as network topology, growth projections, and organizational requirements to determine the optimal subnetting scheme. Command example: "show ip route" to display the routing table, including the subnetted routes. By carefully planning and implementing subnetting techniques, organizations can design a scalable and efficient network infrastructure that meets their current and future needs.

CIDR (Classless Inter-Domain Routing) is another subnetting technique commonly used in modern networks to allocate IP addresses more efficiently. Command example: "ip address 192.168.1.0/24" to specify a CIDR notation for an IP address with a subnet mask of /24. CIDR allows for variable-length subnet masking, enabling finer granularity in address allocation and subnetting. By using CIDR notation, network administrators can simplify subnetting and address allocation, reduce routing table size, and improve network scalability.

In summary, subnetting is a vital networking technique that enables organizations to divide large networks into smaller, more manageable subnetworks. Command example: "show interface vlan" to display the configured VLAN interfaces on a switch. By carefully planning and implementing subnetting techniques, organizations can optimize address space utilization, improve network performance and security, and facilitate network management and troubleshooting. Subnetting calculations require an understanding of binary notation, subnet masks, and the subnetting formula, as well as consideration of factors such as network topology and growth projections.

Chapter 10: Network Troubleshooting Techniques

Diagnosing network issues is a critical skill for network administrators to ensure the smooth operation of computer networks. Command example: "ping" to test network connectivity to a specific host or IP address. Networks are prone to various issues that can disrupt communication and affect productivity, ranging from connectivity problems to performance issues and security breaches. Effective diagnosis of these issues requires a systematic approach, including identifying symptoms, isolating the root cause, and implementing appropriate solutions.

One of the most common network issues is connectivity problems, which can manifest as an inability to access network resources or connect to the internet. Command example: "ipconfig" to display IP configuration information on Windows systems or "ifconfig" on Unix/Linux systems. To diagnose connectivity issues, network administrators can use tools such as ping, traceroute, and nslookup to test connectivity to remote hosts, identify network path delays, and resolve DNS resolution problems.

Ping is a simple yet powerful command-line tool used to verify connectivity between devices on a network. Command example: "ping 192.168.1.1" to ping a specific IP address. By sending ICMP echo requests to a target device and receiving ICMP echo replies, ping can determine whether the target device is reachable and measure round-trip latency. Persistent packet loss or high latency indicates network connectivity issues that may require further investigation.

Traceroute is another useful diagnostic tool for identifying network path delays and routing issues. Command example: "tracert google.com" to trace the route to a remote host. Traceroute sends ICMP or UDP packets with increasing TTL (Time-to-Live) values to trace the path from the source to the destination. Each router along the path decrements the TTL value and forwards the packet until it reaches the destination or the TTL expires. Traceroute displays the IP addresses and round-trip times of each router hop, allowing network administrators to identify bottlenecks or routing loops.

DNS (Domain Name System) resolution issues can also cause connectivity problems, preventing devices from resolving domain names to IP addresses. Command example: "nslookup google.com" to query DNS servers for the IP address of a domain name. Nslookup allows network administrators to troubleshoot DNS resolution problems by querying DNS servers directly and verifying domain name resolution. Failure to resolve domain names or incorrect IP address mappings may indicate DNS configuration issues or DNS server failures.

Another common network issue is performance degradation, which can result from network congestion, bandwidth limitations, or hardware/software issues. Command example: "netstat" to display network statistics and connections on a system. To diagnose performance issues, network administrators can use performance monitoring tools such as netstat,

Wireshark, and SNMP (Simple Network Management Protocol) to analyze network traffic, identify bandwidth-intensive applications, and detect network bottlenecks.

Netstat is a command-line utility that provides information about active network connections, listening ports, and network statistics on a system. Command example: "netstat -an" to display all active TCP connections. By analyzing netstat output, network administrators can identify established connections, monitor network traffic, and detect abnormal network behavior such as excessive connection attempts or port scanning activities.

Wireshark is a powerful network protocol analyzer that captures and displays network packets in real-time. Command example: "wireshark" to launch the Wireshark GUI (Graphical User Interface). Wireshark allows network administrators to capture and analyze network traffic at the packet level, inspect packet headers, and troubleshoot network protocol issues. By examining packet captures, network administrators can identify network errors, protocol mismatches, and performance bottlenecks.

SNMP (Simple Network Management Protocol) is a protocol used for network monitoring and management. Command example: "snmpwalk" to retrieve SNMP information from network devices. SNMP enables network administrators to monitor network devices, collect performance data, and detect network faults remotely. By querying SNMP-enabled devices, network administrators can gather information about device status, interface utilization, and error rates, allowing them to proactively identify and resolve network issues before they impact users.

Security breaches and unauthorized access are also significant concerns for network administrators, requiring vigilant monitoring and threat detection. Command example: "show security firewall" to display firewall configuration and rules. To diagnose security issues, network administrators can use security monitoring tools such as firewalls, intrusion detection systems (IDS), and security information and event management (SIEM) systems to detect and mitigate network threats.

Firewalls are essential network security devices that control and monitor incoming and outgoing network traffic based on predetermined security rules. Command example: "show access-list" to display configured access control lists (ACLs) on a firewall. By inspecting firewall logs and analyzing traffic patterns, network administrators can identify suspicious activities, block malicious traffic, and prevent unauthorized access to network resources.

Intrusion Detection Systems (IDS) are security appliances or software applications that monitor network traffic for signs of malicious activity or policy violations. Command example: "show ip intrusion-detection" to display configured intrusion detection settings. IDS analyzes network packets in real-time, looking for known attack signatures, abnormal behavior, or policy violations. When an intrusion is detected, IDS generates alerts or triggers automated responses to mitigate the threat.

Security Information and Event Management (SIEM) systems are centralized platforms that aggregate and analyze security event logs from various network devices and systems. Command example: "show logging" to display system log messages. SIEM systems correlate security events, detect patterns of suspicious activity, and provide comprehensive visibility into network security posture. By monitoring SIEM alerts and analyzing security event logs, network administrators can identify security breaches, investigate incidents, and implement security controls to protect against future threats.

In summary, diagnosing common network issues requires a combination of troubleshooting tools, command-line utilities, and diagnostic techniques. Command example: "show interface status" to display the status and configuration of network interfaces. By systematically identifying symptoms, isolating the root cause, and implementing appropriate solutions, network administrators can ensure the reliability, performance, and security of computer networks. Continuously monitoring network health, analyzing traffic patterns, and staying informed about emerging threats are essential practices for maintaining a secure and efficient network infrastructure.

Troubleshooting network and system issues is a fundamental aspect of IT support, requiring a combination of diagnostic tools and proven methodologies to identify and resolve problems efficiently. Command example: "ping" to test network connectivity to a specific host or IP address. From network connectivity issues to hardware failures and software glitches, IT professionals rely on various tools and methods to diagnose and rectify problems, ensuring the smooth operation of computer systems and networks.

Ping is perhaps one of the most basic yet essential troubleshooting tools in the IT arsenal, allowing technicians to quickly determine whether a host or device is reachable over the network. Command example: "ping 192.168.1.1" to ping a specific IP address. By sending ICMP echo request packets and waiting for ICMP echo reply packets, ping provides valuable insights into network connectivity and latency, helping technicians pinpoint connectivity issues and potential network bottlenecks.

Traceroute is another indispensable tool for diagnosing network connectivity problems and identifying routing issues. Command example: "traceroute google.com" to trace the route to a remote host. Traceroute works by sending ICMP or UDP packets with increasing TTL (Time-to-Live) values, allowing technicians to trace the path from the source to the destination and identify routers or network segments causing delays or packet loss.

Nslookup is a command-line tool used for querying DNS (Domain Name System) servers to resolve domain names to IP addresses and vice versa. Command example: "nslookup google.com" to query DNS servers for the IP address of a domain name. Nslookup helps technicians diagnose DNS resolution issues, such as incorrect DNS server configuration, DNS cache poisoning, or domain name misspelling, allowing them to troubleshoot and resolve DNS-related problems effectively.

Netstat is a powerful command-line utility for displaying network statistics, active connections, and listening ports on a system. Command example: "netstat -an" to display all active TCP connections. By examining netstat output, technicians can identify established connections, monitor network traffic, and detect abnormal network behavior, such as port scanning or denial-of-service (DoS) attacks, helping them troubleshoot and mitigate network security threats.

Wireshark is a comprehensive network protocol analyzer that captures and displays network packets in real-time. Command example: "wireshark" to launch the Wireshark GUI (Graphical User Interface). Wireshark allows technicians to capture and analyze network traffic at the packet level, inspect packet headers, and troubleshoot network protocol issues, such as packet loss, retransmissions, or protocol mismatches, providing invaluable insights into network performance and behavior.

SNMP (Simple Network Management Protocol) is a protocol used for network monitoring and management, allowing technicians to collect performance data, monitor device status, and detect network faults remotely. Command example: "snmpwalk" to retrieve SNMP information from network devices. SNMP enables technicians to proactively identify and resolve network issues, such as device failures, interface errors, or bandwidth congestion, ensuring the reliability and availability of network resources.

Remote access tools, such as Remote Desktop Protocol (RDP) or SSH (Secure Shell), are essential for troubleshooting and managing remote systems and devices. Command example: "ssh user@hostname" to establish an SSH connection to a remote device. Remote access tools allow technicians to remotely diagnose and resolve problems, configure devices, and perform system maintenance tasks without physical access to the equipment, improving efficiency and minimizing downtime.

Hardware diagnostic tools, such as built-in system diagnostics or third-party hardware testing utilities, are crucial for diagnosing hardware failures and component malfunctions. Command example: "dmesg" to display system messages and kernel logs. By analyzing hardware diagnostic logs, technicians can identify hardware issues, such as faulty memory modules, disk errors, or overheating components, allowing them to replace or repair hardware components as needed.

Software diagnostic tools, such as system monitoring utilities or performance profiling software, are essential for diagnosing software-related issues, such as application crashes, system hangs, or performance degradation. Command example: "top" to display system resource usage and process information. By monitoring system performance metrics, analyzing application logs, and profiling software performance, technicians can identify software bugs, memory leaks, or configuration errors, helping them troubleshoot and resolve software-related problems effectively.

Collaboration and communication tools, such as instant messaging platforms or ticketing systems, play a vital role in troubleshooting by enabling technicians to collaborate with colleagues, share information, and escalate issues as needed. Command example: N/A - collaboration tools are typically web-based or desktop applications that facilitate communication and collaboration among IT teams. By documenting troubleshooting steps, sharing knowledge, and coordinating efforts, technicians can work together to diagnose and resolve complex issues more efficiently, minimizing downtime and improving customer satisfaction.

In summary, troubleshooting tools and methods are essential for diagnosing and resolving a wide range of network and system issues efficiently. Command example: "ipconfig /all" to display detailed IP configuration information on Windows systems. By leveraging diagnostic tools, such as ping, traceroute, Wireshark, and SNMP, and following proven troubleshooting methodologies, technicians can quickly identify the root cause of problems, implement appropriate solutions, and restore normal operation, ensuring the reliability and performance of computer systems and networks. Continuously updating and expanding their troubleshooting toolkit and staying informed about emerging technologies and best practices are essential for IT professionals to effectively address the evolving challenges of modern IT environments.

BOOK 3
ADVANCED DESKTOP SUPPORT STRATEGIES
DEEP DIVE INTO SYSTEM DIAGNOSTICS

ROB BOTWRIGHT

Chapter 1: Understanding System Architecture

Understanding the memory hierarchy and system bus is essential for comprehending the flow of data within a computer system, from the CPU to various levels of memory. Command example: "lshw" to display detailed hardware information on Linux systems or "systeminfo" on Windows systems. The memory hierarchy refers to the organization of different types of memory in a computer system, arranged in levels based on access speed, capacity, and cost. At the heart of the memory hierarchy lies the system bus, a communication pathway that facilitates data transfer between the CPU, memory, and other system components.

The memory hierarchy consists of several levels, each offering different characteristics and serving specific purposes in data storage and retrieval. Command example: "lscpu" to display CPU information on Linux systems or "wmic cpu get caption, deviceid, name, numberofcores, maxclockspeed" on Windows systems. At the top of the memory hierarchy is the CPU cache, a small but ultra-fast memory that stores frequently accessed data and instructions for rapid access by the CPU. The CPU cache is divided into multiple levels, including L1, L2, and L3 caches, each with varying capacities and access speeds. The L1 cache, also known as the primary cache, is the fastest but smallest cache level located directly on the CPU die. Command example: N/A - CPU cache configuration is hardware-specific and not directly controllable via CLI commands. The L1 cache typically consists of separate instruction and data caches, providing low-latency access to frequently used instructions and data. Due to its proximity to the CPU cores, the L1 cache offers the fastest access times but limited capacity, making it suitable for storing critical data for immediate access.

The L2 cache, or secondary cache, is located between the L1 cache and main memory and serves as a larger but slower cache level. Command example: N/A - CPU cache configuration is hardware-specific and not directly controllable via CLI commands. The L2 cache acts as a buffer between the CPU cores and main memory, storing additional data and instructions that cannot fit in the L1 cache. While offering higher capacity than the L1 cache, the L2 cache typically has slightly higher access times, making it suitable for storing moderately accessed data and instructions.

The L3 cache, or last-level cache, is the largest but slowest cache level shared among multiple CPU cores within a processor or across multiple processor cores in a multi-socket system. Command example: N/A - CPU cache configuration is hardware-specific and not directly controllable via CLI commands. The L3 cache serves as a centralized cache pool for storing frequently accessed data and instructions shared among CPU cores, helping improve overall system performance by reducing memory access latency and cache contention.

Beyond the CPU cache, the memory hierarchy includes main memory, also known as RAM (Random Access Memory), which serves as the primary storage medium for program code and data during execution. Command example: "free -h" to display memory usage statistics on Linux systems or "systeminfo" on Windows systems. Main memory offers higher capacity than CPU cache but slower access times, providing a balance between speed and storage capacity. RAM modules are installed on the motherboard and accessed by the CPU via the system bus. The system bus is a communication pathway that connects the CPU, memory, and other system components, facilitating data transfer and communication within the computer system. Command example: "lspci" to display PCI devices on Linux systems or "wmic path Win32_Bus" on Windows systems. The system bus consists of several buses, including the Front Side Bus (FSB), Memory Bus, and Peripheral Component Interconnect (PCI) bus, each serving a specific purpose in data transfer and system communication.

The Front Side Bus (FSB) is a high-speed bus that connects the CPU to the chipset and memory subsystem, allowing the CPU to communicate with main memory and other system components. Command example: N/A - FSB configuration is hardware-specific and not directly controllable via CLI commands. The FSB carries data, address, and control signals between the CPU and memory controller hub (MCH), enabling memory access and data transfer between the CPU and RAM modules.

The Memory Bus, also known as the memory channel or memory interface, is a communication pathway between the CPU and RAM modules, facilitating data transfer and memory access. Command example: N/A - memory bus configuration is hardware-specific and not directly controllable via CLI commands. The memory bus operates at the speed and width of the installed memory modules, allowing the CPU to read from and write to main memory during program execution.

The Peripheral Component Interconnect (PCI) bus is a high-speed expansion bus that connects peripheral devices, such as network adapters, storage controllers, and graphics cards, to the CPU and system memory. Command example: "lspci -v" to display detailed information about PCI devices on Linux systems or "wmic path Win32_PnPEntity" on Windows systems. The PCI bus provides a standardized interface for connecting peripheral devices, allowing for plug-and-play compatibility and expansion of system functionality.

In summary, the memory hierarchy and system bus play crucial roles in facilitating data transfer and communication within a computer system, from the CPU to main memory and peripheral devices. Command example: "dmidecode --type memory" to display memory module information on Linux systems or "wmic memorychip" on Windows systems. By understanding the organization and operation of the memory hierarchy and system bus, computer architects, system administrators, and software developers can design efficient systems, optimize memory performance, and troubleshoot memory-related issues effectively. Continuously monitoring memory usage and system bus performance and upgrading hardware components as needed are essential for maintaining system stability and performance in modern computing environments.

Chapter 2: Advanced Operating System Troubleshooting

In the realm of computer troubleshooting and system maintenance, understanding advanced boot options and recovery tools is paramount for addressing various issues that may arise during system startup and operation. Command example: "msconfig" on Windows systems or "grub-editenv" on Linux systems. Advanced boot options provide users with a range of diagnostic and repair tools that can help resolve issues such as startup failures, system crashes, and corrupted system files.

One of the primary advanced boot options is Safe Mode, a diagnostic mode that loads the operating system with minimal drivers and services, allowing users to troubleshoot issues related to software conflicts or problematic drivers. Command example: "msconfig" on Windows systems allows users to access Safe Mode by configuring the boot options. Safe Mode is particularly useful for troubleshooting issues that occur during system startup or when encountering errors that prevent normal operation.

Another useful advanced boot option is Last Known Good Configuration, which restores the system to a previous state where it last booted successfully. Command example: N/A - Last Known Good Configuration is accessed during the Windows startup process by pressing the F8 key. This option can be helpful in reverting system changes that may have caused instability or system errors, allowing users to restore functionality without losing data or reinstalling the operating system.

The Recovery Console is a command-line interface provided by Windows operating systems that allows users to perform advanced troubleshooting and repair tasks. Command example: "chkdsk" to check and repair disk errors or "sfc /scannow" to scan and repair system files. The Recovery Console can be accessed either from the Windows installation disc or by selecting the Repair Your Computer option during system startup. From the Recovery Console, users can perform tasks such as repairing the Master Boot Record (MBR), restoring system files, and running diagnostic utilities.

System Restore is a feature available in Windows operating systems that allows users to revert the system to a previous restore point, effectively undoing changes that may have caused system instability or errors. Command example: N/A - System Restore is accessed through the System Protection tab in the System Properties window on Windows systems. Users can create restore points manually or allow Windows to create them automatically before system changes, such as software installations or driver updates. System Restore can help restore system functionality without affecting personal files or data.

The Boot Configuration Data (BCD) store is a critical component of the Windows boot process that stores boot configuration parameters and controls how the operating system boots. Command example: "bcdedit" to view and modify BCD settings or "bootrec

/rebuildbcd" to rebuild the BCD store. If the BCD store becomes corrupted or misconfigured, it can result in startup failures or boot errors. Using tools such as bcdedit or bootrec, users can repair the BCD store and restore normal boot functionality.

In addition to advanced boot options provided by the operating system, there are third-party bootable recovery tools available that can help diagnose and repair system issues. Command example: "fdisk -l" on Linux systems to list available disk partitions or "testdisk" to recover lost partitions and repair disk errors. These tools typically run from a bootable USB drive or CD/DVD and offer a range of features for disk management, data recovery, and system repair. Examples include EaseUS Partition Master, TestDisk, and Hiren's BootCD.

On Linux systems, advanced boot options may vary depending on the distribution and boot loader used. Command example: "grub-editenv" on systems using the GRUB bootloader to edit boot parameters or "systemctl rescue.target" to boot into rescue mode. Linux users can access recovery options such as single-user mode, which boots the system into a root shell with minimal services running, allowing users to perform system maintenance tasks or troubleshoot issues.

In summary, advanced boot options and recovery tools are essential components of any computer troubleshooting toolkit, providing users with the means to diagnose and repair a wide range of system issues. Command example: "msconfig" on Windows systems or "grub-editenv" on Linux systems. Whether dealing with startup failures, system crashes, or corrupted files, having access to advanced boot options and recovery tools can help users restore system functionality, recover lost data, and maintain system stability. By familiarizing themselves with these tools and techniques, users can effectively troubleshoot and resolve system issues, minimizing downtime and ensuring smooth operation of their computer systems.

When a computer system encounters a kernel panic or system crash, it can be a distressing experience for users and a challenging issue for system administrators to resolve. Kernel panics occur when the operating system's kernel detects an unrecoverable error or inconsistency that prevents it from continuing normal operation, leading to a system crash or freeze. Command example: "dmesg" to display kernel messages or "sysctl kernel.panic" to configure the kernel panic behavior on Linux systems. Understanding how to debug kernel panics and system crashes is crucial for diagnosing the underlying causes and restoring system stability.

One of the first steps in debugging kernel panics and system crashes is to gather information about the error and its context. Command example: "dmesg" on Linux systems or "Event Viewer" on Windows systems to view system logs and error messages. These logs often contain valuable information about the events leading up to the crash, including error codes, stack traces, and timestamps. By examining the system logs, administrators can gain insight into the nature of the problem and identify potential causes.

Analyzing memory dumps is another essential aspect of debugging kernel panics and system crashes. Command example: "crash" on Linux systems or "Windbg" on Windows systems to analyze memory dumps. When a system crashes, it may generate a memory dump, also known as a core dump or crash dump, which contains a snapshot of the system's memory at the time of the crash. Analyzing memory dumps can help identify the specific code or driver responsible for the crash and pinpoint the root cause of the issue.

Identifying problematic hardware or drivers is often a key step in resolving kernel panics and system crashes. Command example: "lspci" on Linux systems or "Device Manager" on Windows systems to list installed hardware devices. Faulty hardware components, such as RAM modules, hard drives, or expansion cards, can cause system instability and crashes. Similarly, outdated or incompatible device drivers can lead to kernel panics and system crashes. By reviewing the list of installed hardware and drivers, administrators can identify potential culprits and take corrective action.

Performing hardware diagnostics and stress tests can help identify underlying hardware issues that may be contributing to kernel panics and system crashes. Command example: "memtest86" to perform memory diagnostics or "chkdsk" to check disk integrity. Memory tests, such as Memtest86 or Windows Memory Diagnostic, can help identify faulty RAM modules by scanning for errors and inconsistencies. Similarly, disk checks, such as chkdsk on Windows systems or fsck on Linux systems, can detect and repair disk errors that may be causing system crashes.

Updating system software and drivers is essential for maintaining system stability and preventing kernel panics and system crashes. Command example: "apt-get update && apt-get upgrade" on Debian-based Linux systems or "Windows Update" on Windows systems to install software updates. Manufacturers regularly release updates and patches to address security vulnerabilities, fix bugs, and improve compatibility with hardware and software. By keeping the operating system, drivers, and firmware up to date, administrators can minimize the risk of kernel panics and system crashes caused by known issues.

Isolating software conflicts or misconfigurations is another important aspect of debugging kernel panics and system crashes. Command example: "msconfig" on Windows systems or "systemctl" on Linux systems to manage startup services and processes. Conflicting software applications, incorrect configuration settings, or incompatible system tweaks can destabilize the system and lead to crashes. By disabling unnecessary startup programs, services, and system modifications, administrators can identify and resolve conflicts that may be causing kernel panics and system crashes.

Examining hardware temperature and system resource usage can help identify potential causes of kernel panics and system crashes. Command example: "sensors" to monitor hardware temperatures or "top" to view system resource usage on Linux systems. Overheating components, such as the CPU or GPU, can trigger thermal shutdowns or hardware failures that manifest as kernel panics or system crashes. Likewise, excessive system resource usage, such as high CPU or memory utilization, can lead to system instability and crashes. By monitoring hardware temperatures and system resource usage, administrators can proactively identify and address potential issues before they escalate into crashes.

In summary, debugging kernel panics and system crashes requires a systematic approach that involves gathering diagnostic information, analyzing memory dumps, identifying problematic hardware or drivers, performing hardware diagnostics and stress tests, updating system software and drivers, isolating software conflicts or misconfigurations, and monitoring hardware temperature and system resource usage. By following these steps and leveraging appropriate diagnostic tools and techniques, administrators can effectively diagnose the root causes of kernel panics and system crashes, implement corrective actions, and restore system stability. Continuously monitoring system health and addressing potential issues promptly can help minimize downtime and ensure the reliable operation of computer systems in various environments.

Chapter 3: Memory Management and Optimization

Memory allocation algorithms play a crucial role in managing memory resources efficiently within a computer system. Command example: "malloc" in C programming to allocate memory dynamically. These algorithms determine how memory is allocated to processes and how it is reclaimed when no longer needed, ensuring optimal utilization of available memory and preventing issues such as fragmentation and memory leaks. Understanding different memory allocation algorithms is essential for system developers, administrators, and programmers to design and implement robust and efficient memory management systems.

One of the most common memory allocation algorithms is the First Fit algorithm, which allocates the first available block of memory that is large enough to accommodate the requested size. Command example: N/A - First Fit is a strategy commonly implemented in memory allocation libraries and operating systems. When a process requests memory, the allocator searches for the first available block of memory that meets the size requirements and allocates it to the process. While the First Fit algorithm is simple and easy to implement, it may lead to fragmentation over time, as smaller memory blocks become scattered throughout the memory space.

The Best Fit algorithm allocates the smallest block of memory that is large enough to accommodate the requested size, minimizing wasted memory and fragmentation. Command example: N/A - Best Fit is another strategy commonly used in memory allocation systems. When a process requests memory, the allocator searches for the smallest available block of memory that can satisfy the request. While the Best Fit algorithm helps reduce fragmentation and maximize memory utilization, it may result in slower allocation times and increased overhead due to the need to search for the optimal block.

The Worst Fit algorithm allocates the largest available block of memory that is large enough to accommodate the requested size, potentially leading to increased fragmentation but faster allocation times. Command example: N/A - Worst Fit is less commonly used than First Fit or Best Fit due to its tendency to fragment memory space more rapidly. When a process requests memory, the allocator searches for the largest available block of memory that meets the size requirements and allocates it to the process. While the Worst Fit algorithm may result in faster allocation times, it can lead to suboptimal memory utilization and increased fragmentation over time.

The Next Fit algorithm is similar to the First Fit algorithm but starts searching for available memory blocks from the last allocated block, reducing fragmentation and improving allocation efficiency. Command example: N/A - Next Fit is a variation of the First Fit algorithm that is commonly used in memory allocation systems. When a process requests memory, the allocator starts searching for available memory blocks from the last allocated block and continues searching until it finds a suitable block. This approach helps reduce fragmentation by allocating memory blocks closer together, improving overall memory utilization.

The Buddy System is a memory allocation algorithm that divides memory into fixed-size blocks and allocates memory in powers of two sizes, reducing fragmentation and simplifying memory management. Command example: N/A - The Buddy System is a widely used memory allocation technique, particularly in operating systems and embedded systems. When a process requests memory, the allocator searches for the smallest available block that can accommodate the requested size, splitting larger blocks into smaller ones if necessary. By organizing memory into power-of-two-sized blocks and maintaining a free list of available blocks, the Buddy System minimizes fragmentation and overhead while providing efficient memory allocation.

The Slab Allocation algorithm is a memory allocation technique commonly used in Linux-based operating systems to manage kernel memory efficiently. Command example: N/A - Slab Allocation is specific to the Linux kernel and is not directly invoked through a command line interface. Slab Allocation organizes memory into caches of fixed-size memory chunks, or "slabs," which are preallocated and reused to reduce memory fragmentation and overhead. When a kernel data structure needs memory, the allocator searches for an appropriate slab in the cache and allocates memory from it. By grouping similar data structures together and reusing memory slabs, Slab Allocation improves memory utilization and performance in the Linux kernel. In summary, memory allocation algorithms are essential components of modern computer systems, governing how memory resources are managed and utilized. Command example: "malloc" in C programming or "free" to release dynamically allocated memory. By understanding different memory allocation strategies such as First Fit, Best Fit, Worst Fit, Next Fit, Buddy System, and Slab Allocation, system developers and administrators can design and implement efficient memory management systems that minimize fragmentation, prevent memory leaks, and optimize memory utilization. Continuously evaluating and refining memory allocation algorithms based on system requirements and workload characteristics can help ensure the reliable and efficient operation of computer systems in various environments.

Memory leaks are a common issue in software development, where a program fails to release memory it has allocated, leading to a gradual depletion of available memory resources and potential system instability. Command example: "valgrind" on Linux systems or "Xcode Instruments" on macOS systems to detect memory leaks in C/C++ programs. Detecting and preventing memory leaks is crucial for maintaining the reliability and performance of software applications, particularly in long-running or mission-critical environments. Various techniques and tools are available to help developers identify, diagnose, and mitigate memory leaks effectively.

One of the primary techniques for memory leak detection is using specialized debugging tools and profilers that monitor memory usage and identify potential memory leaks in software applications. Command example: "valgrind" on Linux systems is a widely used tool for detecting memory leaks and other memory-related issues in C/C++ programs. Valgrind performs dynamic analysis of program execution, tracking memory allocations and deallocations and detecting memory leaks by identifying blocks of memory that are not properly released. By running the program under Valgrind's supervision, developers can identify memory leaks and pinpoint their source with detailed error messages and stack traces.

Another approach to memory leak detection is manual code inspection and static analysis, where developers review the source code of an application to identify potential memory leaks and address them proactively. Command example: N/A - Manual code inspection involves reviewing the source code of a software application to identify memory allocation and deallocation operations and ensuring that memory is properly managed throughout the program's execution. Developers look for common memory management mistakes, such as forgetting to release allocated memory or referencing freed memory, and apply best practices to prevent memory leaks, such as using smart pointers or automatic memory management techniques.

Memory leak detection can also be performed through automated testing and continuous integration processes, where software applications are subjected to a battery of tests that include memory leak detection as part of the test suite. Command example: N/A - Automated testing frameworks such as Jenkins or Travis CI can be configured to include memory leak detection tests as part of the build and deployment pipeline. By running automated tests that simulate real-world usage scenarios and monitor memory usage, developers can detect memory leaks early in the development lifecycle and address them before they impact production environments.

Dynamic memory analysis tools, such as memory profilers and heap analyzers, are invaluable for detecting memory leaks in complex software applications by providing insights into memory usage patterns and identifying potential memory leaks. Command example: "Xcode Instruments" on macOS systems includes a suite of performance analysis tools, including the Allocations instrument, which can be used to monitor memory allocations and identify memory leaks in Objective-C and Swift applications. By instrumenting the application code and collecting runtime performance data, developers can analyze memory usage behavior and detect memory leaks with precision.

Memory leak prevention starts with adopting best practices and coding standards for memory management, such as using RAII (Resource Acquisition Is Initialization) patterns, smart pointers, and automatic memory management techniques to ensure that memory is properly managed and released throughout the program's lifecycle. Command example: N/A - Memory leak prevention involves incorporating memory management best practices into the software development process, such as using RAII patterns in C++ to automatically manage resource lifetimes and prevent memory leaks. By adopting coding standards that emphasize proper memory management and using language features and libraries that facilitate automatic memory cleanup, developers can minimize the risk of memory leaks in their applications.

Another strategy for memory leak prevention is implementing robust error handling and resource cleanup mechanisms to ensure that memory is released properly in exceptional conditions, such as when an error occurs or a resource becomes unavailable. Command example: N/A - Error handling and resource cleanup are essential aspects of software development that involve designing code paths to handle unexpected conditions gracefully and release resources, including memory, in a timely manner. By implementing error handling mechanisms that catch and handle exceptions and using resource management techniques such as RAII, developers can prevent memory leaks caused by unhandled errors or resource leaks.

Memory leak prevention also involves rigorous testing and code review processes to identify and address memory leaks early in the development lifecycle. Command example: N/A - Code reviews and testing are essential practices in software development that involve reviewing code changes and performing tests to ensure that software meets quality and reliability standards. By incorporating memory leak detection tests into the testing process and conducting thorough code reviews that include memory management best practices, developers can identify and address memory leaks before they impact end-users.

In summary, memory leak detection and prevention are essential aspects of software development that require a combination of tools, techniques, and best practices. Command example: "valgrind" on Linux systems or "Xcode Instruments" on macOS systems can be used to detect memory leaks in C/C++ programs. By leveraging debugging tools, static analysis, automated testing, dynamic memory analysis, and memory management best practices, developers can identify, diagnose, and mitigate memory leaks effectively, ensuring the reliability, performance, and stability of software applications in various environments. Continuously improving memory management practices and incorporating memory leak detection and prevention into the software development lifecycle can help minimize the risk of memory leaks and optimize memory usage in software applications.

Chapter 4: Disk Management and Storage Solutions

Disk partitioning is the process of dividing a physical disk into multiple logical sections or partitions, each of which can be independently managed and used for storing data or installing operating systems. Command example: "fdisk" or "gdisk" on Linux systems to create and manage disk partitions. Effective disk partitioning is essential for organizing and managing storage resources efficiently, optimizing performance, and ensuring data security and integrity. Various partitioning strategies and techniques are available to meet different requirements and use cases, ranging from basic disk partitioning schemes to more advanced setups tailored for specific needs.

One common disk partitioning strategy is to use a single partition for the entire disk, known as a single partition or whole disk partitioning scheme. Command example: "fdisk /dev/sda" to create a single partition on the entire disk "/dev/sda". This approach is simple and straightforward, making it suitable for basic use cases where only one operating system or data storage area is required. However, it may not be optimal for systems that require separate partitions for different purposes, such as separating system files from user data or isolating critical data from less important files.

Another popular partitioning strategy is to divide the disk into multiple partitions, each serving a specific purpose or containing different types of data. Command example: "fdisk /dev/sda" to create multiple partitions on the disk "/dev/sda", such as a root partition ("/"), a swap partition, and a separate partition for user data ("/home"). This partitioning scheme allows for more flexibility and organization, enabling users to allocate storage resources based on their requirements and preferences. For example, separating system files from user data can improve system stability and make it easier to upgrade or reinstall the operating system without affecting personal files.

A variation of the multiple partitioning strategy is to use logical volume management (LVM) to manage disk partitions dynamically, enabling users to resize, move, and create partitions on-the-fly without rebooting the system or losing data. Command example: "lvcreate" and "lvextend" to create and extend logical volumes in an LVM setup. LVM provides advanced features such as volume snapshots, thin provisioning, and striping, making it ideal for environments with changing storage requirements or where flexibility and scalability are paramount. By abstracting physical disk partitions into logical volumes, LVM simplifies disk management and enhances storage efficiency.

Another partitioning strategy is to use disk mirroring or RAID (Redundant Array of Independent Disks) to create redundant copies of data across multiple disks, improving data availability and fault tolerance. Command example: "mdadm" on Linux systems to create and manage software RAID arrays. RAID configurations, such as RAID 1 (mirroring) or RAID 5 (striping with parity), distribute data and parity information across multiple disks to protect against disk failures and data loss. By replicating data across redundant disks, RAID provides data redundancy and fault tolerance, ensuring that data remains accessible even if one or more disks fail.

For systems with specific performance requirements, such as high-speed data access or low-latency storage, partitioning strategies such as disk striping or disk caching can be employed to optimize disk performance. Command example: "mdadm" to create a RAID 0 (striping) array for improved disk read/write performance. Disk striping distributes data across multiple disks in parallel, enabling faster data access and improved throughput. Similarly, disk caching techniques, such as using solid-state drives (SSDs) as cache devices for frequently accessed data, can enhance disk performance by accelerating read/write operations and reducing latency.

In environments where data security and privacy are paramount, disk encryption can be used to protect sensitive information from unauthorized access or data breaches. Command example: "cryptsetup" to create an encrypted volume on a disk partition. Disk encryption techniques, such as using LUKS (Linux Unified Key Setup) or BitLocker on Windows systems, encrypt data stored on disk partitions, making it unreadable without the decryption key. By encrypting sensitive data at rest, disk encryption helps prevent unauthorized access and safeguard confidentiality, integrity, and privacy.

Additionally, partition alignment is a critical consideration when creating disk partitions to ensure optimal performance and compatibility with storage devices, particularly solid-state drives (SSDs) and advanced storage technologies. Command example: N/A - Partition alignment involves aligning the starting sector of disk partitions with the underlying storage device's physical block size, ensuring efficient data access and minimizing unnecessary read-modify-write operations. Misaligned partitions can lead to performance degradation and reduce the lifespan of SSDs, making proper partition alignment essential for maximizing storage performance and longevity.

In summary, disk partitioning strategies play a vital role in organizing and managing storage resources effectively, optimizing performance, and ensuring data security and integrity. Command example: "fdisk", "gdisk", "mdadm", "cryptsetup", and "lvcreate" are commonly used commands for creating and managing disk partitions and RAID arrays. By selecting the appropriate partitioning scheme and techniques based on specific requirements and use cases, users can optimize storage utilization, improve system performance, and enhance data protection in various computing environments. Continuously evaluating and adjusting disk partitioning strategies based on evolving needs and technologies can help ensure efficient and reliable storage management over time.

RAID, or Redundant Array of Independent Disks, is a technology used to combine multiple physical disk drives into a single logical unit for improved performance, fault tolerance, and data redundancy. The configuration and management of RAID arrays are essential tasks for system administrators and storage professionals to ensure data availability, reliability, and performance. Command example: "mdadm" is a commonly used command-line tool on Linux systems for configuring and managing software RAID arrays. Understanding the various RAID levels, configuration options, and management techniques is crucial for optimizing storage resources and maintaining data integrity in RAID environments.

One of the primary considerations when configuring a RAID array is selecting the appropriate RAID level based on performance, redundancy, and capacity requirements. Command example: "mdadm --create /dev/md0 --level=1 --raid-devices=2 /dev/sdb1 /dev/sdc1" to create a RAID 1 (mirroring) array with two disks (/dev/sdb1 and /dev/sdc1). RAID levels, such as RAID 0 (striping), RAID 1 (mirroring), RAID 5 (striping with parity), and RAID 10 (striping and mirroring), offer different combinations of performance, fault tolerance, and usable capacity. By evaluating the specific needs of the system and workload, administrators can choose the optimal RAID level to meet their requirements.

RAID configuration involves setting up the RAID array, initializing disks, defining RAID levels, and configuring array parameters such as chunk size, stripe width, and parity distribution. Command example: "mdadm --create /dev/md0 --level=5 --raid-devices=3 --chunk=64 /dev/sdb1 /dev/sdc1 /dev/sdd1" to create a RAID 5 array with a chunk size of 64 KB and three disks (/dev/sdb1, /dev/sdc1, and /dev/sdd1). Proper configuration ensures optimal performance, fault tolerance, and data protection in RAID environments, maximizing the benefits of RAID technology.

Once the RAID array is configured, ongoing management and monitoring are necessary to ensure its continued operation and reliability. Command example: "mdadm --detail /dev/md0" to display detailed information about the RAID array /dev/md0, including its status, RAID level, member devices, and health. Monitoring tools such as mdadm, SMART (Self-Monitoring, Analysis, and Reporting Technology), and system logs provide insights into array status, disk health, and potential issues that require attention. Regular monitoring and proactive maintenance help prevent data loss and minimize downtime due to disk failures or other RAID-related issues.

RAID management tasks include adding or removing disks from the array, replacing failed disks, rebuilding arrays, and resizing arrays to accommodate changing storage requirements. Command example: "mdadm --add /dev/md0 /dev/sde1" to add a new disk (/dev/sde1) to the RAID array /dev/md0. When a disk fails or becomes unreliable, administrators must replace it promptly to maintain data integrity and array performance. Command example: "mdadm --remove /dev/md0 /dev/sdf1" to remove a failed disk (/dev/sdf1) from the RAID array /dev/md0 and initiate a rebuild process with a replacement disk.

In addition to software RAID, hardware RAID controllers offer advanced features and performance optimizations for managing RAID arrays in enterprise environments. Command example: N/A - Hardware RAID controllers typically provide a web-based management interface or a command-line interface for configuring and monitoring RAID arrays. Hardware RAID controllers offload RAID processing tasks from the host CPU, improving performance and scalability, and often include features such as hot-swappable drive support, cache memory, and battery backup units for data protection.

RAID arrays can also be expanded or migrated to different RAID levels to accommodate changing storage requirements or improve performance and fault tolerance. Command example: "mdadm --grow /dev/md0 --raid-devices=4 --level=5" to migrate a RAID 1 array (/dev/md0) to RAID 5 with four disks. Array expansion involves adding additional disks to the array and redistributing data across the new disks, while migration involves changing the RAID level and restructuring the array accordingly. Proper planning and execution are essential to ensure data integrity and minimize downtime during expansion or migration processes.

Data backup and recovery strategies are critical for protecting data stored on RAID arrays against accidental deletion, corruption, or catastrophic failures. Command example: N/A - Data backup involves regularly backing up critical data stored on RAID arrays to external storage devices or remote backup servers. In the event of data loss or array failure, backups can be used to restore data and minimize downtime. RAID arrays should not be considered a substitute for data backup, as they provide redundancy and fault tolerance but do not protect against data loss due to other factors such as human error or software bugs.

In summary, RAID configuration and management are essential tasks for ensuring data availability, reliability, and performance in storage environments. Command example: "mdadm", SMART monitoring tools, and hardware RAID management interfaces are commonly used for configuring, monitoring, and managing RAID arrays. By selecting the appropriate RAID level, properly configuring arrays, monitoring array health, and implementing proactive maintenance practices, administrators can maximize the benefits of RAID technology and maintain data integrity and availability in diverse computing environments. Continuously evaluating and optimizing RAID configurations based on evolving storage requirements and technologies helps ensure efficient and reliable storage management over time.

Chapter 5: Advanced System Performance Tuning

Monitoring the performance of computer systems, networks, and applications is essential for ensuring optimal operation, identifying bottlenecks, and troubleshooting issues. Command example: "top" command in Linux displays real-time information about system processes, CPU usage, and memory utilization. Performance monitoring tools provide insights into resource utilization, system health, and application performance through various metrics and visualization techniques. By collecting and analyzing performance data, administrators can proactively manage resources, optimize performance, and enhance user experience.

One of the primary objectives of performance monitoring is to identify resource bottlenecks and optimize resource utilization to improve system responsiveness and efficiency. Command example: "vmstat" command in Linux provides detailed statistics about system memory, CPU, disk, and I/O activity. By monitoring key performance metrics such as CPU utilization, memory usage, disk I/O, and network traffic, administrators can pinpoint areas of resource contention and take corrective actions to alleviate bottlenecks and improve overall system performance.

CPU utilization is a critical performance metric that measures the percentage of CPU time spent executing user and system processes. Command example: "mpstat" command in Linux displays CPU usage statistics for each processor core. High CPU utilization can indicate processor saturation and potential performance degradation, leading to sluggish system response times and decreased throughput. By monitoring CPU utilization and identifying processes consuming excessive CPU resources, administrators can optimize CPU allocation, prioritize critical tasks, and improve overall system responsiveness.

Memory utilization is another important performance metric that measures the amount of physical and virtual memory used by system processes and applications. Command example: "free" command in Linux displays information about system memory usage, including total memory, used memory, free memory, and swap space. High memory usage can lead to system slowdowns, excessive paging/swapping, and decreased application performance. By monitoring memory usage and identifying memory-intensive processes, administrators can optimize memory allocation, tune virtual memory settings, and prevent memory-related performance issues.

Disk I/O performance is critical for ensuring efficient data access and storage operations in computer systems and storage environments. Command example: "iostat" command in Linux provides disk I/O statistics, including disk utilization, throughput, and response times. Slow disk I/O can lead to sluggish application performance, increased latency, and degraded system responsiveness. By monitoring disk I/O metrics and identifying disks with high utilization or latency, administrators can optimize disk access patterns, balance I/O loads, and improve overall storage performance.

Network performance monitoring is essential for maintaining network reliability, throughput, and responsiveness in distributed computing environments.

Command example: "iftop" command in Linux displays real-time network traffic statistics, including bandwidth usage, packet counts, and connections. Network congestion, packet loss, and latency can degrade network performance and impact application responsiveness. By monitoring network traffic and analyzing network performance metrics, administrators can identify network bottlenecks, optimize network configurations, and ensure optimal data transfer rates.

Application performance monitoring (APM) tools enable administrators to monitor and analyze the performance of software applications and services in real-time. Command example: N/A - APM tools typically provide graphical interfaces and dashboards for monitoring application performance metrics such as response time, throughput, error rates, and resource utilization. By monitoring application performance metrics and analyzing transaction traces, administrators can identify performance bottlenecks, troubleshoot application issues, and optimize application performance for end-users.

Server uptime and availability are critical for ensuring continuous access to IT services and resources. Command example: "uptime" command in Linux displays system uptime, load averages, and current time. Monitoring server uptime and availability metrics such as uptime percentage, downtime events, and mean time to recovery (MTTR) helps administrators track system reliability, identify potential failures, and implement proactive measures to minimize downtime and service disruptions.

In summary, performance monitoring tools and metrics play a vital role in maintaining the health, efficiency, and reliability of computer systems, networks, and applications. Command example: "sar" command in Linux collects, reports, and analyzes system activity and performance metrics over time. By leveraging performance monitoring tools and analyzing performance metrics, administrators can identify performance bottlenecks, optimize resource utilization, and ensure optimal system performance and user experience. Continuously monitoring and optimizing performance is essential for meeting service level agreements (SLAs), maximizing productivity, and delivering high-quality IT services in dynamic and evolving computing environments.

Optimizing system resources for maximum performance is a critical task for administrators seeking to ensure efficient operation and responsiveness of their computing environments. In today's fast-paced digital landscape, where demands on system resources continue to increase, achieving optimal performance requires a combination of proactive resource management, tuning, and monitoring techniques. By leveraging various tools and methodologies, administrators can identify performance bottlenecks, fine-tune system configurations, and optimize resource utilization to enhance overall system performance.

One of the primary areas of focus when optimizing system resources is the CPU, or Central Processing Unit, which serves as the brain of the computer and executes instructions from software programs. Command example: "top" is a command-line utility commonly used on Unix-like operating systems to display real-time information about CPU usage, memory usage, and running processes.

Monitoring CPU utilization helps administrators identify processes that consume excessive CPU resources and may cause performance degradation. Techniques such as process prioritization, CPU affinity settings, and workload balancing can be employed to optimize CPU usage and improve system responsiveness.

Memory, or RAM (Random Access Memory), is another critical resource that directly impacts system performance. Command example: "free -m" displays information about available memory and swap space on Linux systems. Monitoring memory usage helps administrators identify memory-intensive processes and potential memory leaks that can lead to system slowdowns or instability. Techniques such as memory profiling, caching strategies, and optimizing virtual memory settings can help maximize available memory resources and improve overall system performance.

Storage performance is a key consideration for system optimization, as disk I/O (Input/Output) operations can significantly affect system responsiveness and application performance. Command example: "iostat" is a command-line tool available on Unix-like operating systems that provides detailed statistics about disk I/O activity, including disk throughput, I/O wait times, and disk utilization. Monitoring disk I/O metrics helps administrators identify storage bottlenecks and optimize disk performance through techniques such as RAID configuration, disk partitioning, and filesystem optimization.

Network performance optimization is essential for systems that rely on network connectivity for communication and data transfer. Command example:

"netstat" is a command-line utility used to display network connections, routing tables, and network interface statistics on Unix-like operating systems. Monitoring network traffic and performance metrics helps administrators identify network bottlenecks, optimize network settings, and troubleshoot connectivity issues. Techniques such as Quality of Service (QoS) configuration, network bandwidth management, and optimizing TCP/IP parameters can improve network performance and reliability.

In addition to monitoring system resources, administrators can employ various tuning techniques to optimize system performance further. Command example: "sysctl" is a command-line tool used to modify kernel parameters and system settings on Unix-like operating systems. By adjusting kernel parameters such as process scheduling policies, memory allocation thresholds, and network buffer sizes, administrators can fine-tune system behavior to better match workload requirements and improve performance.

Virtualization technologies such as VMware, Hyper-V, and KVM provide additional opportunities for optimizing system resources through resource pooling, workload consolidation, and dynamic resource allocation. Command example: N/A - Virtualization platforms typically include graphical management interfaces or command-line tools for configuring and managing virtualized environments. By leveraging features such as CPU and memory overcommitment, storage deduplication, and live migration, administrators can optimize resource utilization and improve overall system performance in virtualized environments.

Performance monitoring tools and metrics play a crucial role in optimizing system resources by providing insights into system behavior, resource utilization patterns, and performance bottlenecks. Command example: "sar" (System Activity Reporter) is a command-line utility available on Unix-like operating systems that collects, reports, and archives system activity metrics, including CPU, memory, disk, and network usage. By analyzing performance metrics collected by tools such as sar, administrators can identify areas for improvement, implement targeted optimizations, and measure the impact of tuning efforts on system performance.

Continuous monitoring and optimization of system resources are essential practices for maintaining peak performance and responsiveness in dynamic computing environments. Command example: "perf" is a command-line performance analysis tool available on Linux systems that provides detailed insights into CPU, memory, and software performance. By regularly monitoring system performance, identifying performance bottlenecks, and applying optimization techniques, administrators can ensure that systems operate efficiently and deliver optimal performance for users and applications.

Chapter 6: Malware Detection and Removal Techniques

Advanced malware analysis methods are indispensable for cybersecurity professionals in comprehensively understanding and mitigating sophisticated threats. In today's complex threat landscape, where malware continues to evolve in sophistication and stealthiness, employing advanced analysis techniques is essential for accurately identifying, analyzing, and responding to malicious code. By leveraging a combination of static and dynamic analysis approaches, reverse engineering techniques, and specialized tools, analysts can gain deep insights into malware behavior, uncover its functionality, and develop effective countermeasures to protect systems and networks from cyber threats.

Static analysis is a fundamental technique used to examine malware without executing it, providing insights into its structure, characteristics, and potential capabilities. Command example: "strings" is a command-line utility that extracts printable strings from binary files, helping analysts identify text-based indicators such as hardcoded URLs, filenames, and cryptographic keys embedded within malware binaries. By analyzing file headers, metadata, and code sections, analysts can determine the file type, identify suspicious artifacts, and extract embedded resources such as executables, scripts, or configuration files for further analysis.

Dynamic analysis involves executing malware in a controlled environment, such as a virtual machine or sandbox, to observe its behavior and interactions with the system. Command example: "procmon" (Process Monitor) is a command-line tool available on Windows systems that monitors system activity in real-time, including file system and registry changes, process creations, and network activity. By running malware samples in a sandboxed environment and monitoring system activity with tools like procmon, analysts can observe malicious behavior, such as file drops, registry modifications, network connections, and process injections, to understand the malware's functionality and potential impact on the system.

Behavioral analysis focuses on understanding malware's actions and impact on the compromised system, helping analysts identify malicious activities and assess the severity of the threat. Command example: "volatility" is a command-line tool used for memory forensics analysis, allowing analysts to extract and analyze volatile data from memory dumps. By examining process memory, network connections, and system artifacts, analysts can identify indicators of compromise (IOCs), such as suspicious processes, network communications, or modifications to system configuration, enabling them to assess the scope and severity of the malware infection.

Code analysis, also known as reverse engineering, involves dissecting malware binaries to understand their internal logic, functionality, and evasion techniques. Command example: "IDA Pro" is a disassembler and debugger tool commonly used for reverse engineering malware binaries. By analyzing assembly code, function calls, and control flow graphs, analysts can reverse engineer malware to uncover its algorithms, encryption routines, and command-and-control (C2) communication protocols, facilitating the development of detection signatures and mitigation strategies.

Malware sandboxing is a technique used to execute suspicious files in an isolated environment to analyze their behavior and assess their impact on the system without risking infection. Command example: "Cuckoo Sandbox" is an open-source malware analysis platform that automates the execution of malware samples in a virtualized environment and provides detailed reports on their behavior. By submitting suspicious files to a sandbox environment, analysts can observe their execution, monitor system activity, and analyze network traffic to identify malicious behavior and potential indicators of compromise.

Memory forensics analysis involves examining the contents of system memory to identify malicious processes, injected code, and artifacts left behind by malware. Command example: "Volatility" is a command-line tool used for memory forensics analysis, allowing analysts to extract and analyze volatile data from memory dumps. By analyzing memory dumps captured from infected systems, analysts can identify malware processes, uncover rootkits, and extract volatile artifacts such as process memory, network connections, and registry keys, providing valuable insights into the malware's behavior and impact on the compromised system.

Network traffic analysis is a critical aspect of malware analysis, allowing analysts to monitor and analyze network communications to identify malicious behavior and detect command-and-control (C2) activities. Command example: "Wireshark" is a packet analyzer tool that captures and displays network traffic in real-time, allowing analysts to inspect packets, filter traffic, and analyze protocols. By capturing and analyzing network traffic associated with malware infections, analysts can identify malicious domains, IP addresses, and communication patterns, enabling them to block malicious traffic and disrupt C2 communications.

Dynamic malware analysis involves executing malware samples in a controlled environment to observe their behavior and interactions with the system. Command example: "sandbox" is a command-line tool that creates a virtualized environment for executing malware samples in isolation. By running malware samples in a sandbox environment, analysts can observe their behavior, monitor system activity, and analyze malicious activities such as file drops, registry modifications, and network connections, providing valuable insights into the malware's functionality and capabilities.

Threat intelligence feeds and repositories provide analysts with access to curated datasets of known malware samples, indicators of compromise (IOCs), and behavioral patterns, enabling them to identify and analyze emerging threats. Command example: "MISP" (Malware Information Sharing Platform) is an open-source threat intelligence platform that allows organizations to share and collaborate on threat intelligence data. By integrating threat intelligence feeds into their analysis workflows, analysts can identify malware samples, extract IOCs, and correlate threat data to enhance their understanding of evolving threats and improve their ability to detect and respond to cyber attacks.

In summary, advanced malware analysis methods are essential for effectively combating sophisticated cyber threats and protecting systems and networks from malicious activities. By leveraging a combination of static and dynamic analysis techniques, reverse engineering methodologies, and specialized tools, analysts can gain deep insights into malware behavior, uncover its functionality, and develop effective mitigation strategies to defend against cyber attacks. Continuous research, training, and collaboration within the cybersecurity community are crucial for staying abreast of evolving threats and adapting analysis techniques to address emerging challenges in malware detection and response.

Implementing behavioral analysis for malware detection is a crucial aspect of modern cybersecurity strategies, enabling organizations to detect and mitigate advanced threats that evade traditional signature-based antivirus solutions. Behavioral analysis focuses on observing and analyzing the behavior of software applications and processes to identify suspicious or malicious activities indicative of malware presence. By monitoring various system events, file modifications, network communications, and process behaviors, security analysts can detect and respond to malware infections in real-time, enhancing overall threat detection capabilities and reducing the risk of data breaches and system compromise.

One effective technique for implementing behavioral analysis is through the use of sandbox environments. Command example: "Cuckoo Sandbox" is an open-source automated malware analysis system that provides a virtualized environment for executing and observing the behavior of suspicious files and programs. By running suspicious files within isolated sandbox environments, security analysts can monitor their behavior, including file system modifications, registry changes, network communications, and process interactions, without risking the integrity of the host system. Sandboxing allows analysts to execute malware samples in a controlled environment, enabling them to observe and analyze malicious behaviors without exposing their organization's network to potential harm.

Another approach to behavioral analysis involves the use of network traffic monitoring and analysis tools. Command example: "Wireshark" is a popular network protocol analyzer that captures and analyzes network traffic in real-time. By monitoring network communications at the packet level, security analysts can identify suspicious patterns, anomalies, or malicious activities indicative of malware infections. Behavioral indicators such as unusual traffic patterns, communication with known malicious IP addresses, or unexpected protocol usage can signal the presence of malware within the network. Network-based behavioral analysis complements endpoint-based approaches by providing insights into malware activities that may evade detection at the endpoint level.

Command example: "Process Monitor" (procmon) is a Windows Sysinternals tool that monitors system activity, including file system and registry operations, process creation, and network activity. By capturing and analyzing system events in real-time, Process Monitor enables security analysts to track the behavior of running processes and identify potentially malicious activities indicative of malware infections. Process Monitor provides detailed insights into process behavior, allowing analysts to correlate suspicious events with known malware behaviors and indicators of compromise (IOCs). By leveraging Process Monitor's filtering and logging capabilities, analysts can focus on relevant system events and quickly identify and respond to malware threats.

Additionally, security information and event management (SIEM) platforms play a vital role in behavioral analysis by aggregating and correlating security events from various sources across the enterprise network. Command example: "Splunk" is a leading SIEM solution that collects, indexes, and analyzes log data from diverse sources, including security appliances, servers, endpoints, and applications. By correlating security events and log data from multiple sources, Splunk enables security analysts to detect and investigate potential security incidents, including malware infections, data breaches, and insider threats. By leveraging Splunk's advanced analytics and machine learning capabilities, organizations can detect and respond to malware threats more effectively, reducing the dwell time and mitigating the impact of security breaches.

Furthermore, machine learning and artificial intelligence (AI) techniques are increasingly being employed to enhance behavioral analysis capabilities and improve malware detection accuracy. Command example: "TensorFlow" is an open-source machine learning framework that enables developers to build and deploy machine learning models for various tasks, including malware detection. By training machine learning models on large datasets of known malware samples and benign software, security analysts can develop predictive models that can automatically identify and classify malware based on behavioral features and patterns. Machine learning-based behavioral analysis enables organizations to detect previously unseen malware variants and zero-day threats, enhancing overall threat detection capabilities and reducing false positives.

In summary, implementing behavioral analysis for malware detection is essential for organizations seeking to defend against advanced and evolving cyber threats. By leveraging sandbox environments, network traffic monitoring tools, endpoint monitoring solutions, SIEM platforms, and machine learning techniques, organizations can enhance their ability to detect and respond to malware infections in real-time, reducing the risk of data breaches and minimizing the impact of security incidents. Behavioral analysis provides a proactive approach to cybersecurity that complements traditional signature-based antivirus solutions, enabling organizations to stay ahead of emerging threats and protect their critical assets and data from malicious actors.

Chapter 7: System Recovery and Backup Strategies

Disaster recovery planning and implementation is a critical aspect of ensuring business continuity and minimizing the impact of unforeseen events on organizational operations. In today's digital landscape, where organizations rely heavily on IT systems and data for their day-to-day operations, the need for robust disaster recovery strategies has never been more apparent. Command example: "rsync" is a command-line utility used for file synchronization and data backup on Unix-like systems. By establishing comprehensive disaster recovery plans and implementing effective mitigation measures, organizations can mitigate the risk of data loss, downtime, and financial loss in the event of disasters.

Disasters come in various forms, including natural disasters such as earthquakes, floods, and hurricanes, as well as human-made disasters like cyberattacks, hardware failures, and data breaches. Command example: "tar" is a command-line utility used for archiving files on Unix-like systems. Regardless of the nature of the disaster, having a well-defined disaster recovery plan in place is essential for organizations to minimize disruptions, maintain service levels, and protect their reputation and brand image.

The first step in disaster recovery planning is conducting a comprehensive risk assessment to identify potential threats and vulnerabilities that could impact business operations. Command example: "nmap" is a command-line network scanning tool used for discovering hosts and services on a computer network. By assessing risks and prioritizing critical assets and systems, organizations can develop tailored disaster recovery plans that address specific threats and vulnerabilities.

Once risks have been identified, organizations can begin developing disaster recovery strategies and procedures to mitigate the impact of potential disasters. Command example: "dd" is a command-line utility used for disk cloning and imaging on Unix-like systems. Disaster recovery strategies may include data backup and replication, redundant infrastructure deployment, failover mechanisms, and offsite data storage solutions.

Data backup and recovery are fundamental components of any disaster recovery plan, enabling organizations to restore critical data and systems in the event of data loss or corruption. Command example: "scp" is a command-line utility used for securely copying files between hosts on a network. Organizations can implement regular data backup routines, automated backup solutions, and incremental backup strategies to ensure data integrity and availability.

In addition to data backup, organizations should also consider implementing redundancy and failover mechanisms to maintain service availability in the event of hardware or software failures. Command example: "keepalived" is a command-line utility used for implementing high availability solutions on Unix-like systems. Redundant hardware components, load balancing, and clustering techniques can help minimize downtime and ensure continuous service delivery.

Offsite data storage is another critical component of disaster recovery planning, enabling organizations to maintain copies of critical data and systems in geographically diverse locations. Command example: "rsync" with SSH can be used to securely synchronize data between local and remote systems. By storing backups offsite, organizations can protect against localized disasters such as fires, floods, or theft that may impact primary data centers.

Testing and validation are essential aspects of effective disaster recovery planning, ensuring that recovery procedures work as intended and meet business requirements. Command example: "curl" is a command-line tool used for transferring data from or to a server, supporting various protocols. Organizations should conduct regular disaster recovery drills, tabletop exercises, and simulation tests to evaluate the effectiveness of their recovery plans and identify areas for improvement.

Continuous monitoring and maintenance are necessary to keep disaster recovery plans up to date and aligned with evolving business needs and technological advancements. Command example: "cron" is a command-line utility used for scheduling tasks on Unix-like systems. Organizations should regularly review and update their disaster recovery plans, conduct risk assessments, and incorporate lessons learned from past incidents to enhance resilience and readiness.

By following best practices for disaster recovery planning and implementation, organizations can minimize the impact of disasters on their operations, protect critical assets and data, and ensure business continuity in the face of adversity. Command example: "iptables" is a command-line utility used for configuring firewall rules on Unix-like systems. Investing in robust disaster recovery strategies and solutions is essential for safeguarding the long-term viability and success of organizations in today's unpredictable and rapidly evolving business environment.

Backup and restore best practices are essential for ensuring the integrity, availability, and recoverability of critical data and systems in the face of data loss, corruption, or system failures. In today's data-driven world, where organizations rely heavily on digital assets for their day-to-day operations, implementing effective backup and restore strategies is paramount. Command example: "tar" is a command-line utility used for creating compressed archive files on Unix-like systems. By following established best practices and leveraging advanced backup and restore techniques, organizations can minimize the risk of data loss, maintain compliance with regulatory requirements, and safeguard their business continuity.

One of the foundational principles of backup and restore best practices is implementing a comprehensive backup strategy that covers all critical data and systems. Command example: "rsync" is a command-line utility used for file synchronization and data transfer on Unix-like systems. Organizations should identify and prioritize critical data and systems for backup, considering factors such as data importance, frequency of change, and recovery time objectives (RTOs) and recovery point objectives (RPOs).

Regular backups are essential for maintaining data integrity and recoverability, enabling organizations to restore data to a previous state in the event of data loss or corruption. Command example: "rsnapshot" is a command-line backup utility that uses rsync and hard links to create incremental backups on Unix-like systems. Organizations should establish backup schedules based on data sensitivity and business requirements, ensuring that backups are performed regularly and consistently.

Implementing a combination of full backups, incremental backups, and differential backups can help optimize backup storage space and reduce backup window durations. Command example: "cp" is a command-line utility used for copying files and directories on Unix-like systems. Full backups capture entire datasets, while incremental backups and differential backups only capture changes since the last backup, reducing backup storage requirements and backup duration.

Offsite backups are critical for protecting data against localized disasters such as fires, floods, or theft that may impact primary data centers. Command example: "scp" is a command-line utility used for securely copying files between hosts on a network. Organizations should store backup copies in geographically diverse locations, either physically or in the cloud, to ensure data redundancy and resilience in the face of disasters.

Encryption plays a crucial role in securing backup data during transmission and storage, protecting sensitive information from unauthorized access or data breaches. Command example: "gpg" is a command-line encryption tool used for encrypting and decrypting files on Unix-like systems. Organizations should encrypt backup data both in transit and at rest, using strong encryption algorithms and encryption keys to ensure data confidentiality and integrity.

Regular testing and validation of backup and restore procedures are essential for ensuring that backup data is recoverable and meets business requirements. Command example: "md5sum" is a command-line utility used for calculating and verifying checksums on Unix-like systems. Organizations should conduct regular backup integrity checks, file-level checksum verifications, and restoration tests to validate backup data integrity and recoverability.

Retention policies define how long backup data should be retained and when it should be deleted or archived. Command example: "find" is a command-line utility used for searching files and directories on Unix-like systems. Organizations should establish retention policies based on regulatory requirements, business needs, and data lifecycle considerations, ensuring that backup data is retained for an appropriate duration and disposed of securely when no longer needed.

Versioning backups allow organizations to maintain multiple versions of backup data, enabling them to restore data to specific points in time and recover from data corruption or unintended changes. Command example: "rsnapshot" with versioning enabled creates snapshots of backup data at different points in time, allowing organizations to roll back to previous versions if necessary. Versioning backups provide additional protection against ransomware attacks and data tampering, ensuring data recoverability and integrity.

By implementing backup and restore best practices, organizations can mitigate the risk of data loss, maintain data availability and integrity, and ensure business continuity in the face of unforeseen events. Command example: "bacula" is a command-line backup software suite that provides advanced backup and restore capabilities on Unix-like systems. Investing in robust backup and restore solutions and adhering to established best practices are essential for safeguarding critical data and systems and maintaining organizational resilience in today's dynamic and data-centric business environment.

Chapter 8: Virtualization and Containerization Technologies

Hypervisor types and deployment models are integral components of virtualization technologies, revolutionizing the way organizations manage their IT infrastructure and resources. Hypervisors, also known as virtual machine monitors (VMMs), play a crucial role in enabling virtualization by abstracting physical hardware resources and creating virtual environments called virtual machines (VMs) or guests. These virtualized environments enable organizations to consolidate workloads, improve resource utilization, and enhance scalability and flexibility across their IT infrastructure.

There are two primary types of hypervisors: Type 1 (bare-metal) hypervisors and Type 2 (hosted) hypervisors. Type 1 hypervisors run directly on the physical hardware without the need for an underlying operating system, providing direct access to hardware resources for improved performance and efficiency. Command example: "Xen" is a Type 1 hypervisor commonly used in enterprise environments, providing high-performance virtualization capabilities on Linux-based platforms. Type 2 hypervisors, on the other hand, run atop a conventional operating system and rely on the host OS kernel for hardware access, resulting in slightly degraded performance compared to Type 1 hypervisors. Command example: "VirtualBox" is a Type

2 hypervisor that runs on various operating systems, including Windows, macOS, and Linux, providing easy-to-use virtualization solutions for desktop environments.

Within each hypervisor type, there are different deployment models that organizations can choose based on their specific requirements, infrastructure, and use cases. The two main deployment models are on-premises (private cloud) and cloud-based (public cloud) deployments. On-premises deployments involve hosting hypervisor infrastructure and virtualized environments within an organization's own data center, providing full control, customization, and security over the virtualization environment. Command example: "VMware vSphere" is an enterprise-grade virtualization platform used for on-premises deployments, offering advanced features such as high availability, fault tolerance, and distributed resource scheduling. Cloud-based deployments, on the other hand, leverage third-party cloud service providers' infrastructure to host virtualized environments, enabling organizations to access scalable resources on-demand without the need for upfront infrastructure investment. Command example: "Amazon EC2" is a cloud computing platform offered by Amazon Web Services (AWS), allowing users to deploy and manage virtual servers in the cloud using a variety of instance types and configurations.

Furthermore, within cloud-based deployments, there are different service models known as Infrastructure as a Service (IaaS), Platform as a Service (PaaS), and Software as a Service (SaaS). IaaS providers offer virtualized infrastructure resources such as virtual machines, storage, and networking, allowing organizations to deploy and manage their own virtualized environments. Command example: "Microsoft Azure Virtual Machines" is an IaaS offering from Microsoft Azure, providing scalable and customizable virtual machine instances on-demand. PaaS providers offer higher-level services built on top of virtualized infrastructure, such as databases, application development platforms, and middleware, simplifying application deployment and management for developers and organizations. Command example: "Google App Engine" is a PaaS offering from Google Cloud Platform (GCP), allowing developers to build and deploy scalable web applications without managing underlying infrastructure. SaaS providers deliver fully functional software applications over the internet on a subscription basis, eliminating the need for organizations to install, maintain, and manage software locally. Command example: "Salesforce" is a SaaS CRM (Customer Relationship Management) platform that enables organizations to manage customer relationships, sales, and marketing activities through a web-based interface.

In addition to deployment models, there are different virtualization use cases and scenarios where hypervisors are deployed to address specific business needs and requirements. Command example: "KVM" (Kernel-based Virtual Machine) is a Type 1 hypervisor that is integrated into the Linux kernel, providing open-source virtualization solutions for Linux-based environments.

Virtualization use cases include server consolidation, where multiple virtual machines are hosted on a single physical server to maximize resource utilization and reduce hardware costs. Command example: "VMware ESXi" is a bare-metal hypervisor designed for server virtualization, enabling organizations to consolidate workloads, improve server efficiency, and streamline management tasks. Other use cases include desktop virtualization, where virtual desktop infrastructure (VDI) solutions are deployed to provide users with remote access to virtual desktop environments from any device, anywhere. Command example: "Citrix Virtual Apps and Desktops" is a VDI solution that allows organizations to deliver virtualized Windows applications and desktops to end-users securely and efficiently.

Moreover, hypervisors play a critical role in enabling cloud computing and digital transformation initiatives, empowering organizations to embrace agile, scalable, and cost-effective IT solutions. Command example: "OpenStack" is an open-source cloud computing platform that utilizes hypervisor technology to orchestrate and manage virtualized resources across private and public cloud environments. By leveraging hypervisors and virtualization technologies, organizations can accelerate application development and deployment, improve business agility, and drive innovation across their IT infrastructure.

Overall, hypervisor types and deployment models are fundamental concepts in virtualization technology, providing organizations with the flexibility, scalability, and efficiency required to meet the demands of modern

IT environments. Command example: "Oracle VM VirtualBox" is a cross-platform virtualization software that allows users to create and manage virtual machines on desktop computers, providing a versatile and user-friendly virtualization solution for development, testing, and experimentation purposes. Whether deployed on-premises or in the cloud, hypervisors play a central role in enabling organizations to optimize resource utilization, enhance operational efficiency, and drive business growth in today's dynamic and competitive digital landscape.

Docker and Kubernetes are two popular technologies widely used for containerization and container orchestration, respectively. Understanding their deployment strategies is essential for efficiently managing and scaling containerized applications in modern IT environments.

Docker provides a platform for developing, shipping, and running applications in lightweight, portable containers. These containers encapsulate all the dependencies required for an application to run consistently across different environments. Docker deployment strategies involve various techniques for building, distributing, and managing Docker containers.

One of the fundamental Docker deployment strategies is the use of Dockerfiles, which are text files containing instructions for building Docker images. These instructions specify the base image, environment variables, dependencies, and commands needed to configure and run the application within the container.

Command example: **docker build -t myapp .** This command builds a Docker image named "myapp" using the Dockerfile located in the current directory.

Once Docker images are built, they can be stored in Docker registries, such as Docker Hub or private registries, for distribution and sharing among developers and deployment environments. Command example: **docker push myapp** This command pushes the Docker image named "myapp" to the default Docker registry.

For deploying Docker containers in production environments, Docker Compose is a popular tool used to define and manage multi-container applications. Docker Compose uses YAML files to specify the services, networks, and volumes required for running the application. Command example: **docker-compose up -d** This command starts the services defined in the Docker Compose file in detached mode, allowing them to run in the background.

Additionally, Docker Swarm is a built-in orchestration tool in Docker Engine that enables the deployment and management of containerized applications across a cluster of Docker hosts. Docker Swarm utilizes the concept of services to define the desired state of an application, including the number of replicas and placement constraints. Command example: **docker service create --name myservice myapp** This command creates a Docker service named "myservice" using the Docker image "myapp."

On the other hand, Kubernetes, often abbreviated as K8s, is an open-source container orchestration platform designed to automate the deployment, scaling, and management of containerized applications. Kubernetes deployment strategies focus on defining and managing Kubernetes resources, such as pods, deployments, services, and ingresses, to ensure the efficient operation of containerized workloads.

One of the primary Kubernetes deployment strategies is the use of Kubernetes manifests, which are YAML or JSON files describing the desired state of Kubernetes resources. Kubernetes manifests define the configuration, specifications, and relationships between different components of an application. Command example: **kubectl apply -f myapp.yaml** This command applies the Kubernetes manifest file "myapp.yaml" to create or update Kubernetes resources.

Kubernetes also supports various deployment techniques, such as rolling updates and blue-green deployments, to ensure zero-downtime updates and smooth transitions between different versions of an application. Rolling updates gradually replace old instances of an application with new ones, allowing for seamless updates without service interruption. Command example: **kubectl apply -f myapp-new.yaml --record** This command applies the updated manifest file "myapp-new.yaml" with the --record flag to track the deployment history.

Similarly, blue-green deployments involve running two identical production environments, blue and green, and switching traffic from one environment to another after a new version is deployed and tested. Kubernetes ingress controllers can be used to manage traffic routing and load balancing between different environments. Command example: **kubectl apply -f ingress.yaml** This command applies the Kubernetes Ingress manifest file to define routing rules for directing traffic to the blue or green environment.

Moreover, Kubernetes provides advanced features such as horizontal pod autoscaling (HPA) and cluster autoscaling to dynamically scale resources based on workload demand. HPA automatically adjusts the number of pod replicas based on CPU or memory utilization metrics, while cluster autoscaling scales the underlying infrastructure to accommodate increased resource demands. Command example: **kubectl autoscale deployment myapp --cpu-percent=80 --min=1 --max=10** This command creates an HPA for the deployment "myapp," targeting 80% CPU utilization and scaling between 1 and 10 replicas.

In summary, Docker and Kubernetes offer powerful deployment strategies for containerized applications, allowing organizations to build, deploy, and scale applications efficiently in modern cloud-native environments. By leveraging Dockerfiles, Docker Compose, Docker Swarm, Kubernetes manifests, and advanced Kubernetes features, organizations can streamline their application deployment processes, improve resource utilization, and achieve greater agility and scalability in their IT operations.

Chapter 9: Deep Dive into Diagnostic Tools and Utilities

Advanced system monitoring tools play a crucial role in maintaining the health, performance, and stability of IT infrastructures. These tools provide deep insights into various aspects of system behavior, resource utilization, and application performance, enabling administrators to detect issues, troubleshoot problems, and optimize system performance. One such tool is Nagios, a popular open-source monitoring solution used for monitoring IT infrastructure components such as servers, switches, routers, and services. Nagios uses a plugin-based architecture to collect data from different sources and provides alerts and notifications based on predefined thresholds. Administrators can use the **check_nrpe** command to execute Nagios Remote Plugin Executor (NRPE) plugins on remote hosts and retrieve performance data.

Another widely used system monitoring tool is Zabbix, an open-source monitoring software known for its scalability and flexibility. Zabbix allows administrators to monitor various metrics such as CPU usage, memory utilization, network traffic, and disk space across multiple platforms and operating systems. Administrators can use the Zabbix Agent to collect data from monitored hosts and send it to the Zabbix server for processing and analysis. The **zabbix_get** command can be used to retrieve specific values from monitored hosts, while the **zabbix_sender** command can be used to send custom data to the Zabbix server for monitoring.

Prometheus is another powerful monitoring tool commonly used in cloud-native environments for monitoring containerized applications and microservices. Prometheus employs a pull-based model for collecting metrics, where it scrapes data from instrumented targets at regular intervals. Administrators can use Prometheus Query Language (PromQL) to query and analyze collected metrics, perform alerting based on predefined rules, and visualize data using Grafana, a popular open-source dashboarding tool. With Prometheus, administrators can monitor various aspects of containerized environments, including resource usage, application performance, and service health.

In addition to these open-source solutions, there are commercial system monitoring tools available in the market, such as SolarWinds Orion and Dynatrace, which offer advanced features and capabilities for monitoring complex IT environments. SolarWinds Orion provides comprehensive monitoring and alerting capabilities for network devices, servers, virtualization platforms, and cloud services. Administrators can use the SolarWinds web console to configure monitoring templates, set up alerting thresholds, and visualize performance data using customizable dashboards. Similarly, Dynatrace is an AI-driven monitoring solution that leverages artificial intelligence and machine learning algorithms to automatically detect and diagnose performance issues across hybrid cloud environments. Dynatrace offers real-time visibility into application dependencies, transaction traces, and user experiences, helping organizations ensure optimal performance and reliability of their digital services.

Furthermore, modern system monitoring tools often integrate with other IT management solutions such as IT service management (ITSM) platforms, configuration management databases (CMDBs), and incident management systems to provide end-to-end visibility and streamline IT operations. For example, tools like ServiceNow and BMC Helix integrate with monitoring tools to automatically generate incidents, create tickets, and initiate remediation workflows based on predefined conditions and alerting rules. This integration enhances collaboration between IT teams, improves incident response times, and minimizes service disruptions.

Moreover, with the rise of cloud computing and DevOps practices, observability has become a critical aspect of modern system monitoring. Observability refers to the ability to understand how systems behave internally based on external inputs and outputs. Tools like Datadog and New Relic offer comprehensive observability solutions that enable organizations to monitor and trace distributed systems, analyze application logs and traces, and gain insights into the performance and behavior of complex architectures. These tools help organizations proactively identify performance bottlenecks, troubleshoot issues, and optimize system performance to meet business objectives.

In summary, advanced system monitoring tools play a vital role in modern IT operations by providing real-time visibility, actionable insights, and proactive monitoring capabilities across diverse IT environments. Whether open-source or commercial, these tools empower administrators to monitor infrastructure components, applications, and services effectively, detect anomalies and performance issues, and ensure the reliability and performance of digital services. By leveraging advanced monitoring tools and practices, organizations can enhance their operational efficiency, reduce downtime, and deliver superior user experiences to their customers.

System profiling and tracing techniques are indispensable tools in the arsenal of system administrators and developers alike, offering insights into the behavior and performance of software and hardware components. Profiling involves analyzing the execution of a program or system to identify bottlenecks, resource utilization patterns, and areas for optimization. One commonly used profiling tool is **perf**, a powerful Linux performance analysis tool that provides a wide range of features for profiling CPU, memory, and I/O performance. With **perf**, administrators can collect detailed performance data, including CPU cycles, cache misses, and instruction counts, to pinpoint performance issues and optimize system performance. For example, the command **perf record** can be used to collect performance data for a specific command or application, while **perf report** can be used to analyze the collected data and identify performance bottlenecks.

Another popular profiling tool is **gprof**, which is used for profiling C and C++ programs to identify hotspots in code execution. **gprof** works by instrumenting the code with profiling hooks and collecting data on function call frequencies and execution times. Administrators can then use the **gprof** command to generate a profile report, which provides insights into the execution flow of the program and highlights functions that consume the most CPU time. By optimizing these hotspots, developers can improve the overall performance of their applications.

In addition to CPU profiling, memory profiling is also essential for identifying memory leaks, heap allocations, and inefficient memory usage patterns. Valgrind is a powerful memory profiling tool widely used for detecting memory-related errors and issues in C and C++ programs. Valgrind works by running the program in a virtual environment and instrumenting memory operations to detect errors such as memory leaks, buffer overflows, and uninitialized memory accesses. Administrators can use the **valgrind** command to analyze the memory behavior of a program and identify memory-related issues that could lead to crashes or security vulnerabilities.

Furthermore, system tracing techniques provide visibility into the runtime behavior of applications and system components, allowing administrators to trace the execution flow, monitor system calls, and diagnose performance issues. **strace** is a commonly used system call tracing tool available on Linux systems, which intercepts and records system calls made by a process. Administrators can use **strace** to monitor file system operations, network communication, and inter-process communication, helping diagnose issues such as file access errors, permission problems, and system call failures. For example, the command **strace -p <pid>** can be used to attach **strace** to a running process and trace its system calls in real-time.

Moreover, **dtrace** is a dynamic tracing framework available on some Unix-like operating systems, including Solaris, macOS, and FreeBSD, which allows administrators to instrument and trace system behavior in real-time. **dtrace** provides a powerful scripting language that enables administrators to define custom tracing probes, collect data from various system components, and analyze system behavior dynamically. With **dtrace**, administrators can monitor CPU utilization, disk I/O latency, and application performance metrics, enabling them to diagnose performance issues and optimize system performance effectively.

Additionally, **ebpf** (extended Berkeley Packet Filter) is an advanced tracing framework available on Linux systems, which allows administrators to trace and analyze kernel and user-space events in real-time. **ebpf** provides a flexible and efficient way to instrument the kernel and user-space programs, allowing administrators to collect detailed performance data and diagnose complex issues. Using **bpftrace**, a high-level tracing language for **ebpf**, administrators can write custom tracing scripts to monitor various aspects of system behavior, such as CPU usage, disk I/O activity, and network traffic, enabling them to gain deep insights into system performance and behavior.

Furthermore, distributed tracing tools such as Jaeger and Zipkin are essential for monitoring and troubleshooting distributed systems and microservices architectures. These tools provide end-to-end visibility into distributed transactions, enabling administrators to trace requests across multiple services and identify latency bottlenecks and errors. By instrumenting applications with tracing libraries and deploying tracing agents, administrators can collect distributed traces and visualize the flow of requests through the system, helping diagnose performance issues and optimize system performance in distributed environments.

In summary, system profiling and tracing techniques are indispensable tools for analyzing the behavior and performance of software and hardware components. Whether profiling CPU and memory usage, tracing system calls and events, or monitoring distributed transactions, these techniques provide administrators with valuable insights into system behavior, enabling them to diagnose issues, optimize performance, and ensure the reliability and efficiency of their systems. By leveraging profiling and tracing tools effectively, administrators can identify bottlenecks, optimize resource utilization, and deliver high-performance, reliable applications and services to end-users.

Chapter 10: Advanced Network Analysis and Monitoring

Packet analysis with Wireshark is a fundamental skill for network administrators, security analysts, and anyone responsible for troubleshooting network issues or investigating security incidents. Wireshark is a powerful open-source network protocol analyzer that allows users to capture, inspect, and analyze network traffic in real-time. With Wireshark, users can gain deep insights into network communications, identify potential security threats, and diagnose network performance problems.

To start packet analysis with Wireshark, the first step is to capture network traffic. This can be done by running Wireshark on a computer connected to the network interface where the traffic of interest flows. Alternatively, Wireshark can be deployed on a network tap or a SPAN (Switched Port Analyzer) port on a network switch to capture traffic without impacting network performance. Once Wireshark is running, users can initiate a packet capture by selecting the appropriate network interface and clicking on the "Start" button. Wireshark will then begin capturing packets and displaying them in real-time in its main interface.

Once the packet capture is complete, users can start analyzing the captured packets to gain insights into network behavior and diagnose issues. Wireshark provides powerful filtering and search capabilities that allow users to focus on specific packets of interest. For example, users can filter packets based on protocol, source or destination IP address, port number, or other criteria using Wireshark's display filters. The **ip.addr == x.x.x.x** command can be used to filter packets based on IP address, while the **tcp.port == xxxx** command can be used to filter packets based on TCP port number.

In addition to filtering packets, Wireshark also provides various analysis tools and features to help users understand network traffic patterns and behavior. For example, Wireshark's packet dissection feature allows users to view detailed information about each packet, including its protocol headers, payload, and timing information. Users can analyze packet headers to identify the source and destination IP addresses, port numbers, protocol types, and other relevant information.

Wireshark also includes built-in protocol decoders for a wide range of network protocols, allowing users to dissect and analyze packets at a high level. These protocol decoders provide detailed information about the structure and content of network protocols, making it easier to understand the purpose and function of each packet. Users can expand and collapse packet details in Wireshark's packet list and packet details panes to focus on specific aspects of the captured traffic.

One of the key features of Wireshark is its support for advanced analysis tasks such as protocol troubleshooting, performance analysis, and security investigations. Wireshark's expert system provides real-time feedback and analysis of network traffic, highlighting potential issues or anomalies detected in the captured packets. Users can leverage Wireshark's expert system to identify common network problems such as retransmissions, out-of-order packets, and protocol errors.

Moreover, Wireshark supports the decryption of encrypted network traffic for protocols such as SSL/TLS, SSH, and IPsec, allowing users to inspect the contents of encrypted communications. This capability is particularly useful for security analysts investigating potential security incidents or monitoring for malicious activity on the network. By decrypting encrypted traffic, users can identify malicious payloads, command and control communications, and other indicators of compromise.

In addition to real-time packet analysis, Wireshark also supports offline analysis of packet capture files saved in the popular PCAP (Packet Capture) format. Users can open and analyze saved packet capture files in Wireshark, allowing for retrospective analysis of network traffic and historical investigation of security incidents. This offline analysis capability is useful for forensic investigations, incident response, and performance troubleshooting.

Furthermore, Wireshark integrates with other network analysis and security tools, allowing users to share captured packet data and collaborate with colleagues. Wireshark supports the export of packet capture files in various formats, including CSV, JSON, and PDML, for further analysis in other tools or platforms. Additionally, Wireshark can be used in conjunction with intrusion detection systems (IDS), network forensic tools, and SIEM (Security Information and Event Management) platforms to provide comprehensive network visibility and threat detection capabilities.

In summary, Wireshark is a versatile and powerful tool for packet analysis, offering a wide range of features and capabilities for network troubleshooting, performance analysis, and security investigations. Whether capturing packets in real-time or analyzing offline packet capture files, Wireshark provides users with the tools they need to understand network behavior, diagnose issues, and investigate security incidents effectively. By mastering Wireshark's features and techniques, network professionals can become proficient in analyzing network traffic and maintaining the security and reliability of their networks.

Intrusion Detection and Prevention Systems (IDPS) are crucial components of modern cybersecurity frameworks, providing organizations with proactive measures to detect and mitigate potential security threats. Configuring an IDPS involves a series of steps aimed at tailoring the system to the specific needs and security requirements of an organization.

The first step in configuring an IDPS is to select an appropriate deployment model based on the organization's network architecture and security objectives. IDPS can be deployed in various modes, including inline, passive, or hybrid configurations. In an inline deployment, the IDPS sits directly in the network traffic path and can actively block or allow traffic based on predefined rules. Passive deployments, on the other hand, analyze network traffic without directly impacting its flow, making them suitable for monitoring purposes. Hybrid deployments combine elements of both inline and passive modes to provide a balanced approach to intrusion detection and prevention.

Once the deployment model is determined, the next step is to define the scope and objectives of the IDPS configuration. This involves identifying the types of threats and attacks the IDPS will be tasked with detecting and preventing, as well as the specific assets and network segments it will protect. For example, an organization may prioritize the protection of critical servers and sensitive data, requiring the IDPS to focus on monitoring and securing these assets.

With the scope and objectives established, the next step is to configure the IDPS rules and policies to align with the organization's security requirements. This includes defining signatures for known threats, creating custom rules to detect suspicious behavior, and setting thresholds for alerting and blocking actions. Many IDPS solutions offer pre-configured rule sets and templates based on industry best practices, which can serve as a starting point for customization.

In addition to rule configuration, fine-tuning the sensitivity and specificity of the IDPS is essential to minimize false positives and negatives. This involves adjusting parameters such as alert thresholds, correlation rules, and anomaly detection settings to strike a balance between detecting genuine threats and minimizing noise. CLI commands such as **set sensitivity level** or **configure alert threshold** may be used to adjust these parameters, depending on the specific IDPS solution being deployed.

Furthermore, integrating the IDPS with other security tools and systems within the organization's environment is critical for maximizing its effectiveness. This may include integrating with firewall appliances, SIEM platforms, threat intelligence feeds, and endpoint security solutions to share threat information and coordinate response actions. CLI commands such as **configure integration settings** or **set up threat intelligence feed** may be used to configure these integrations.

Another important aspect of IDPS configuration is defining response actions for detected threats. This includes specifying how the IDPS should respond to different types of threats, such as blocking malicious traffic, quarantining compromised devices, or generating alerts for further investigation. CLI commands such as **configure response actions** or **set up automated blocking** may be used to define these response policies.

Once the IDPS configuration is complete, ongoing monitoring and maintenance are essential to ensure its continued effectiveness. This includes regularly reviewing and updating rules and policies to adapt to evolving threats and network conditions, as well as analyzing alerts and incident reports to identify trends and patterns indicative of potential security issues. CLI commands such as **monitor rule effectiveness** or **review incident logs** may be used to perform these tasks.

Additionally, conducting regular security audits and assessments of the IDPS configuration can help identify any weaknesses or gaps in coverage that may need to be addressed. This may involve conducting penetration tests, vulnerability scans, or tabletop exercises to validate the effectiveness of the IDPS in detecting and preventing real-world threats. CLI commands such as **conduct security audit** or **perform vulnerability assessment** may be used to facilitate these activities.

In summary, configuring an Intrusion Detection and Prevention System is a critical component of any comprehensive cybersecurity strategy. By following best practices and leveraging CLI commands and techniques, organizations can deploy an IDPS that effectively detects and mitigates potential security threats, helping to protect sensitive data and preserve the integrity of their networks and systems.

BOOK 4
EXPERT-LEVEL NETWORK TROUBLESHOOTING
PRO TIPS FOR RESOLVING COMPLEX ISSUES

ROB BOTWRIGHT

Chapter 1: Advanced Routing and Switching Protocols

OSPF (Open Shortest Path First) is a widely-used routing protocol in computer networks, known for its scalability, flexibility, and efficiency in determining the best path for data packets. Understanding OSPF involves delving into its intricacies, including its routing algorithm, network topology database, and various configuration options.

At the heart of OSPF is its link-state routing algorithm, which allows routers to exchange information about network topology changes by sharing link-state advertisements (LSAs). These LSAs contain information about router and network interfaces, link costs, and neighboring routers. By collecting and processing LSAs, OSPF routers build a detailed map of the network, enabling them to calculate the shortest path to each destination using Dijkstra's algorithm.

Deploying OSPF begins with configuring OSPF routers to participate in the OSPF routing process. This involves enabling OSPF on router interfaces and assigning each interface to an OSPF area. OSPF areas are logical subdivisions of the network that help improve scalability and reduce routing overhead. CLI commands such as **router ospf [process ID]** and **network [network address] [wildcard mask] area [area ID]** are used to configure OSPF routing on Cisco routers.

Once OSPF is enabled and configured, routers exchange OSPF hello packets to establish neighbor adjacencies and form the OSPF topology database. Neighbor adjacencies are essential for OSPF routers to exchange routing information and synchronize their network databases. CLI commands such as **show ip ospf neighbor** and **show ip ospf database** can be used to verify OSPF neighbor relationships and inspect the OSPF topology database.

One of the key features of OSPF is its support for hierarchical network design through the use of OSPF areas. OSPF areas allow network administrators to partition large networks into smaller, more manageable segments, reducing the amount of routing information exchanged between routers and improving network performance. Areas are connected by OSPF backbone areas, also known as Area 0, which serve as transit areas for interconnecting OSPF areas.

Configuring OSPF areas involves assigning routers and network segments to specific areas based on their logical and geographical proximity. This can be accomplished by specifying the area ID in OSPF configuration commands or by using OSPF area range commands to summarize routes between areas. CLI commands such as **area [area ID] range [network address] [mask]** and **show ip ospf interface** are used to configure and verify OSPF area assignments.

In addition to basic OSPF configuration, network administrators can fine-tune OSPF behavior by adjusting various OSPF parameters and metrics. These parameters include OSPF timers, interface costs, and OSPF authentication settings. CLI commands such as **ip ospf hello-interval, ip ospf cost,** and **ip ospf**

authentication are used to configure OSPF parameters on router interfaces.

Furthermore, OSPF supports multiple types of OSPF network topologies, including point-to-point, broadcast, non-broadcast, and point-to-multipoint. Each OSPF network type has its own characteristics and requirements, such as the need for designated routers (DR) and backup designated routers (BDR) in broadcast networks. CLI commands such as **ip ospf network** and **ip ospf priority** are used to configure OSPF network types and elect DR/BDR routers.

Another important aspect of OSPF configuration is route summarization, which helps reduce the size of OSPF routing tables and minimize routing update overhead. Route summarization involves aggregating multiple network prefixes into a single summary route, which is advertised to neighboring routers. CLI commands such as **ip summary-address** are used to configure route summarization on OSPF routers.

Additionally, OSPF supports various features and mechanisms to enhance network stability and convergence, such as OSPF stub areas, OSPF virtual links, and OSPF authentication. These features allow network administrators to optimize OSPF behavior to meet specific network requirements and security policies. CLI commands such as **area [area ID] stub** and **area [area ID] virtual-link [router ID]** are used to configure OSPF stub areas and virtual links.

In summary, OSPF is a powerful and versatile routing protocol that plays a critical role in modern computer networks. By understanding OSPF's routing algorithm, network topology database, and configuration options, network administrators can deploy OSPF effectively to build scalable and resilient networks.CLI commands and configuration techniques are essential tools for deploying and managing OSPF networks, allowing administrators to fine-tune OSPF behavior and optimize network performance.

BGP (Border Gateway Protocol) is a crucial routing protocol used to exchange routing information between different autonomous systems (AS) on the internet. Implementing BGP involves understanding its features, configuration options, and best practices for optimal routing performance and network reliability.

BGP is unique among routing protocols due to its policy-based routing approach, where routing decisions are based on a variety of attributes such as path length, AS path, and BGP community values. BGP routers exchange routing information, called BGP updates, containing network reachability information and associated attributes. BGP speakers then use this information to build a routing table and make forwarding decisions.

Deploying BGP typically starts with configuring BGP sessions between routers in different ASs. BGP sessions are established between peers using TCP connections, usually over port 179. BGP speakers exchange BGP update messages containing routing information and negotiate parameters such as the BGP version, autonomous system number (ASN), and optional capabilities. The command **neighbor [IP address]**

remote-as [ASN] is used to configure BGP neighbors on Cisco routers.

BGP routers exchange multiple types of BGP messages during the BGP session establishment and maintenance process. These messages include OPEN, UPDATE, KEEPALIVE, and NOTIFICATION messages. The OPEN message initiates the BGP session, while UPDATE messages contain routing information. KEEPALIVE messages maintain the BGP session, and NOTIFICATION messages signal errors or termination of the BGP session.

One of the key considerations in BGP implementation is the design of the BGP routing policy. BGP allows network administrators to implement fine-grained routing policies to influence how traffic flows through the network. These policies can include route filtering, route manipulation, and traffic engineering techniques. CLI commands such as **route-map** and **prefix-list** are used to configure BGP routing policies on Cisco routers.

BGP supports various features and mechanisms to enhance routing stability and scalability, including route aggregation, route reflection, and BGP communities. Route aggregation reduces the size of the BGP routing table by summarizing multiple routes into a single aggregate route. Route reflection simplifies BGP route distribution in large networks by allowing BGP speakers within the same AS to reflect routes without requiring a full mesh of BGP connections.

Furthermore, BGP communities provide a way to tag and manipulate groups of routes for policy enforcement or traffic engineering purposes. BGP communities are optional transitive attributes that can be attached to BGP routes and propagated throughout the network. Network administrators can use BGP communities to implement traffic engineering policies, control route propagation, and signal route preferences to neighboring ASs.

BGP also supports various mechanisms for route filtering and route validation to prevent the propagation of incorrect or malicious routing information. BGP route filtering allows network administrators to selectively advertise or suppress specific routes based on predefined criteria. BGP route validation mechanisms such as RPKI (Resource Public Key Infrastructure) provide a way to cryptographically verify the authenticity of BGP route announcements.

Another important aspect of BGP implementation is route convergence and stability. BGP routers use various mechanisms to ensure fast and stable convergence in response to network topology changes or routing updates. These mechanisms include BGP route dampening, BGP graceful restart, and BGP route refresh. BGP route dampening helps suppress unstable routes to prevent route oscillations and reduce BGP routing table churn.

Moreover, BGP routers exchange BGP route updates using incremental updates, where only changes to routing information are transmitted rather than the entire routing table. This helps reduce bandwidth consumption and improve BGP convergence time. CLI commands such as **clear ip bgp** and **show ip bgp** are used to troubleshoot BGP routing issues and verify BGP neighbor relationships and routing table entries.

In summary, implementing BGP requires careful planning, configuration, and monitoring to ensure optimal routing performance and network reliability. By understanding BGP features, configuration options, and best practices, network administrators can deploy BGP effectively to build scalable and resilient networks. CLI commands play a crucial role in configuring and managing BGP routers, allowing administrators to fine-tune BGP behavior and troubleshoot routing issues efficiently.

Chapter 2: VLANs and Inter-VLAN Routing

VLAN Trunking Protocol (VTP) is a Cisco proprietary protocol used for propagating VLAN configuration information across a network infrastructure. VTP simplifies VLAN management by allowing administrators to configure VLANs on one switch and have those changes automatically propagated to other switches in the same VTP domain. To configure VTP on a Cisco switch, the vtp mode command is used to specify the VTP mode, which can be either server, client, or transparent. In server mode, a switch can create, modify, and delete VLANs, while in client mode, a switch can only receive and synchronize VLAN configuration from VTP servers. Transparent mode allows the switch to forward VTP advertisements but does not participate in VTP updates. Additionally, the vtp domain command is used to set the VTP domain name, which must match on all switches within the same VTP domain to synchronize VLAN information. Once VTP mode and domain are configured, VLANs can be created using the vlan command, and these VLANs will be automatically propagated to other switches in the VTP domain. It's essential to ensure that VTP configuration revision numbers are synchronized across all switches in the VTP domain to prevent unintended VLAN deletions or modifications. To verify VTP configuration and status, the show vtp status command can be used, which displays VTP mode, domain, and revision number information. Additionally, the show vlan brief command can be used to display a summary of VLANs configured on the switch, including VLAN names, VLAN IDs, and associated ports. VTP pruning is a feature that helps optimize bandwidth usage in VLAN-based networks by preventing unnecessary flooding of broadcast, multicast, and unknown unicast traffic to switches that do not have ports in the corresponding VLAN. To enable VTP pruning on a Cisco switch, the vtp pruning command is used in global configuration mode. Once enabled, VTP pruning dynamically prunes VLANs from trunk links where they are not needed, based on VLAN information received from VTP advertisements. It's important to note that VTP pruning is only effective in VTP server mode and should be carefully configured to avoid unintended traffic isolation. While VTP can simplify VLAN management and configuration in network environments, it's essential to understand its limitations and potential risks. For example, VTP advertisements are sent over trunk links, so proper trunk link configuration and security measures must be in place to prevent unauthorized access to VTP domains. Additionally, changes made in one VTP domain will not affect VLAN configurations in other VTP domains, so caution should be exercised when connecting switches from different VTP domains. To mitigate the risk of unintended VLAN modifications or deletions, VTP transparent mode can be used, where VLAN configuration changes are not propagated automatically, and VLANs must be manually configured on each switch. Overall, VTP configuration requires careful planning and monitoring to ensure consistent

VLAN configurations and network stability across all switches in a VTP domain. Inter-VLAN routing is a crucial aspect of network design, allowing communication between different VLANs within the same network infrastructure. Traditionally, VLANs are isolated broadcast domains, meaning devices within one VLAN cannot communicate directly with devices in another VLAN without a router. However, with inter-VLAN routing, traffic can be routed between VLANs, enabling seamless communication across the network.

One common method for implementing inter-VLAN routing is through the use of a Layer 3 switch. Layer 3 switches have routing capabilities built into the hardware, allowing them to route traffic between VLANs without the need for an external router. To configure inter-VLAN routing on a Layer 3 switch, the **interface vlan** command is used to create a virtual interface for each VLAN, assigning an IP address to each interface within the respective VLAN subnet. Additionally, the **ip routing** command must be enabled to activate the routing functionality on the switch. Once configured, the Layer 3 switch can route traffic between VLANs based on destination IP addresses, allowing devices in different VLANs to communicate with each other.

Another approach to inter-VLAN routing is to use a router connected to each VLAN as a gateway. In this scenario, the router acts as the interconnection point between VLANs, routing traffic between them. To configure inter-VLAN routing on a router, subinterfaces are created on the physical interface corresponding to each VLAN, with each subinterface assigned an IP address within the respective VLAN subnet. The router's routing table is then updated to include routes to the VLAN subnets, enabling it to forward traffic between VLANs.

When implementing inter-VLAN routing, several considerations should be taken into account to ensure optimal performance and security. One such consideration is the choice of routing protocol. While static routing can be used for simple network setups, dynamic routing protocols such as Routing Information Protocol (RIP), Open Shortest Path First (OSPF), or Enhanced Interior Gateway Routing Protocol (EIGRP) offer advantages in scalability and automatic route updates.

Additionally, VLAN design plays a crucial role in inter-VLAN routing efficiency. Grouping devices with similar communication requirements into the same VLAN can reduce unnecessary traffic between VLANs and improve network performance. Careful consideration should also be given to subnetting, as each VLAN should have its own subnet to avoid IP address conflicts and ensure proper routing.

Security is another important consideration when implementing inter-VLAN routing. Access control lists (ACLs) can be applied to VLAN interfaces to control the types of traffic allowed to pass between VLANs. For example, ACLs can be used to restrict traffic based on source or destination IP addresses, protocols, or port numbers, helping to enforce network security policies and prevent unauthorized access or malicious activity.

Quality of Service (QoS) mechanisms can also be employed to prioritize certain types of traffic, such as voice or video data, over others to ensure optimal performance for critical applications. This can be achieved by configuring QoS policies on routers or Layer 3 switches to prioritize or limit bandwidth for specific traffic flows.

Monitoring and troubleshooting are essential aspects of managing inter-VLAN routing. Network administrators should regularly monitor traffic patterns and performance metrics to identify potential bottlenecks or issues. Tools such as network analyzers or SNMP monitoring software can provide valuable insights into network traffic and performance. In the event of connectivity issues or performance degradation, troubleshooting techniques such as packet capture, traceroute, or ping can help diagnose and resolve the problem.

Overall, inter-VLAN routing is a fundamental component of modern network design, enabling efficient communication between different network segments. By understanding the various techniques and considerations involved in inter-VLAN routing, network administrators can design and deploy robust and secure networks that meet the needs of their organizations.

Chapter 3: Spanning Tree Protocol (STP) Optimization

Rapid Spanning Tree Protocol (RSTP) is an evolution of the original Spanning Tree Protocol (STP) designed to provide faster convergence and better loop prevention in Ethernet networks. RSTP enhances the STP algorithm by reducing the convergence time when topology changes occur, allowing network devices to adapt quickly to network changes and minimize downtime.

To configure RSTP on network switches, the first step is to access the switch's command-line interface (CLI) using a terminal emulator such as PuTTY or SecureCRT. Once logged in, the administrator can enter privileged EXEC mode by typing the **enable** command and providing the appropriate password. This mode allows the administrator to access configuration commands for the switch.

Next, the administrator must navigate to the global configuration mode by typing the **configure terminal** command. In this mode, the administrator can configure RSTP parameters for the switch. The first RSTP-related command to enter is the **spanning-tree mode rapid-pvst** command, which enables RSTP and sets the switch to use the Rapid PVST+ (Per-VLAN Spanning Tree Plus) mode.

After enabling RSTP, the administrator can configure additional RSTP parameters to optimize network performance. One such parameter is the bridge priority, which determines the priority of the switch in the spanning tree topology. Lower bridge priority values indicate higher priority, with the default value being 32768. To adjust the bridge priority, the administrator can use the **spanning-tree vlan <vlan-id> priority <priority-value>** command, replacing **<vlan-id>** with the VLAN identifier and **<priority-value>** with the desired priority value.

Another important RSTP parameter is the port priority, which determines the priority of individual switch ports in the spanning tree topology. Lower port priority values indicate higher priority, with the default value being 128. To adjust the port priority for a specific interface, the administrator can use the **spanning-tree vlan <vlan-id> port-priority <priority-value>** command, replacing **<vlan-id>** with the VLAN identifier and **<priority-value>** with the desired priority value.

In addition to configuring RSTP parameters, the administrator can also verify the RSTP configuration and monitor the spanning tree topology using various show commands. For example, the **show spanning-tree** command displays the current spanning tree information for all VLANs configured on the switch, including the root bridge, bridge priority, and port roles. Furthermore, the **show spanning-tree vlan <vlan-id>** command provides detailed spanning tree information for a specific VLAN, allowing the administrator to verify the root bridge, designated ports, and port roles within the VLAN. These show commands are invaluable for troubleshooting RSTP-related issues and ensuring the proper functioning of the spanning tree topology.

Overall, configuring RSTP on network switches is essential for optimizing network performance and minimizing downtime due to topology changes. By following the steps outlined above and utilizing the appropriate CLI commands, network administrators can deploy RSTP effectively and ensure the stability and reliability of their Ethernet networks.

Spanning Tree Protocol (STP) is a fundamental mechanism used in Ethernet networks to prevent loops and ensure network stability. At the heart of STP operation lies the concept of the root bridge, which serves as the focal point of the spanning tree topology. The root bridge is responsible for initiating the spanning tree algorithm and determining the shortest path to reach all other switches in the network. As such, the selection of the root bridge is a critical aspect of STP configuration, and adhering to best practices can help optimize network performance and reliability.

To ensure an efficient root bridge election process, network administrators should follow several key best practices. Firstly, it's crucial to strategically position the root bridge within the network topology. Typically, the root bridge should be placed at the core or distribution layer of the network, where it can effectively serve as the central point of connectivity. By placing the root bridge in a central location, administrators can minimize the overall path lengths and optimize traffic flow throughout the network.

In terms of STP configuration, administrators should prioritize switches with higher processing capabilities and ample resources to handle the responsibilities of the root bridge. This often involves selecting switches with superior hardware specifications, such as higher processing power, memory capacity, and forwarding capabilities. By choosing robust switches for the root bridge role, administrators can ensure optimal performance and reliability under various network conditions.

Additionally, administrators should consider configuring the root bridge priority to influence the root bridge election process actively. The root bridge priority value determines the likelihood of a switch being elected as the root bridge, with lower values indicating higher priority. By assigning a lower priority value to the desired root bridge switch, administrators can influence the election outcome and ensure that the most suitable switch assumes the root bridge role.

To configure the root bridge priority, administrators can use the **spanning-tree vlan <vlan-id> root primary** or **spanning-tree vlan <vlan-id> root secondary** commands, where **<vlan-id>** represents the VLAN identifier. The **root primary** command sets the priority value to the lowest possible value, increasing the likelihood of the switch becoming the root bridge. Conversely, the **root secondary** command sets the priority value slightly higher, allowing the switch to become the root bridge only if no other switches have a lower priority.

Furthermore, administrators should implement redundancy and failover mechanisms to ensure network resilience in the event of root bridge failure. Configuring backup root bridge candidates and enabling features such as Rapid Spanning Tree Protocol (RSTP) or Multiple Spanning Tree Protocol (MSTP) can help mitigate the impact of root bridge disruptions and maintain network availability.

Regular monitoring and maintenance of the spanning tree topology are also essential to verify the effectiveness of the root bridge configuration and detect any potential issues. Administrators can use commands such as **show spanning-tree** to view the current spanning tree status and verify the root bridge configuration.

By adhering to these best practices and leveraging appropriate STP configuration commands, network administrators can optimize the root bridge election process and ensure the stability and efficiency of their Ethernet networks.

Chapter 4: Quality of Service (QoS) Implementation

Traffic classification and marking techniques are essential components of network management and quality of service (QoS) implementations. These techniques enable network administrators to identify and prioritize different types of network traffic based on specific criteria, such as application type, source or destination IP address, port numbers, or packet attributes. By classifying and marking traffic, administrators can enforce policies to ensure that critical applications receive the necessary bandwidth and quality of service while preventing network congestion and optimizing performance.

One of the primary methods for traffic classification is through the use of access control lists (ACLs). ACLs allow administrators to define rules that match specific traffic characteristics and assign them to different categories or classes. For example, administrators can create ACLs to classify traffic based on destination IP addresses, source ports, or protocol types. Once classified, traffic can be marked with Differentiated Services Code Point (DSCP) values or Class of Service (CoS) markings to prioritize it within the network.

To implement ACL-based traffic classification and marking, administrators can use the **access-list** command on Cisco devices to create ACLs that match specific traffic criteria. For example, to create an ACL that matches traffic destined for a specific IP address range, the following command can be used:

arduinoCopy code

access-list 100 permit ip any 192.168.1.0 0.0.0.255

This ACL permits traffic destined for the IP address range 192.168.1.0/24. Once the ACL is created, administrators can apply it to the desired interface using the **ip access-group** command:

kotlinCopy code

interface GigabitEthernet0/1 ip access-group 100 in

This command applies ACL 100 to the inbound traffic on interface GigabitEthernet0/1, allowing administrators to classify and mark traffic as it enters the interface.

In addition to ACL-based classification, administrators can also utilize deep packet inspection (DPI) techniques to analyze the contents of network packets and classify traffic based on application signatures or payload content. DPI solutions such as intrusion detection/prevention systems (IDS/IPS) or next-generation firewalls (NGFWs) can identify and categorize traffic based on specific protocols, applications, or user-defined criteria.

Furthermore, network devices such as routers and switches support various QoS mechanisms, including Differentiated Services (DiffServ) and Integrated Services (IntServ), to prioritize and manage traffic based on its classification and marking. DiffServ employs a scalable and flexible approach to QoS by utilizing DSCP values to differentiate between different classes of traffic. Administrators can assign different DSCP values to traffic based on its importance or priority, allowing routers and switches to prioritize critical traffic accordingly.

To configure DiffServ-based QoS, administrators can use the **mls qos** command on Cisco Catalyst switches to enable QoS features and specify the mapping of DSCP values to egress queues. For example, the following

commands configure the switch to trust incoming DSCP values and prioritize traffic based on DSCP markings:
Copy code

mls qos mls qos trust dscp

Additionally, administrators can leverage IntServ mechanisms such as Resource Reservation Protocol (RSVP) to reserve network resources for specific flows or applications, ensuring predictable and guaranteed levels of service. RSVP allows hosts to request bandwidth reservations from network devices along the data path, enabling end-to-end QoS guarantees for critical applications.

Overall, traffic classification and marking techniques play a crucial role in network management and QoS provisioning, allowing administrators to prioritize traffic, enforce policies, and optimize network performance based on specific requirements and business objectives. By employing ACLs, DPI, and QoS mechanisms such as DiffServ and IntServ, administrators can ensure that critical applications receive the necessary bandwidth and quality of service to meet the needs of users and applications across the network.

Queue management and prioritization are critical aspects of quality of service (QoS) implementation in network environments. QoS ensures that network resources are allocated efficiently to meet the requirements of different applications and users, thereby enhancing overall network performance and user experience. Queue management involves organizing and controlling the flow of traffic through network devices, such as routers and switches, while prioritization determines the order in which packets are processed and forwarded based on their importance and the policies defined by administrators.

At the heart of QoS queue management and prioritization are the various queuing mechanisms implemented within network devices. These mechanisms determine how packets are queued and scheduled for transmission based on their classification and priority. One commonly used queuing mechanism is the Weighted Fair Queuing (WFQ) algorithm, which dynamically allocates bandwidth to different flows based on their weights and ensures fairness among competing traffic streams.

To deploy WFQ on Cisco routers, administrators can use the **fair-queue** command under the interface configuration mode. For example, the following command enables WFQ on an interface:

kotlinCopy code

```
interface GigabitEthernet0/0 fair-queue
```

This command configures the router to use WFQ for traffic queuing on interface GigabitEthernet0/0, allowing for fair distribution of bandwidth among different flows.

In addition to WFQ, other queuing mechanisms such as Priority Queuing (PQ), Custom Queuing (CQ), and Class-Based Queuing (CBQ) are also commonly employed to prioritize traffic based on specific criteria. PQ assigns strict priorities to different traffic classes, allowing high-priority traffic to be transmitted ahead of lower-priority traffic. CQ divides traffic into separate queues and assigns each queue a specific amount of bandwidth, while CBQ enables more granular control over traffic prioritization by allowing administrators to define traffic classes based on access control lists (ACLs) or other criteria.

To configure PQ on Cisco routers, administrators can use the **priority-list** command to specify the priority of different traffic classes. For example, the following commands configure PQ with two priority levels:

cssCopy code

```
priority-list 1 protocol ip high list 101 priority-list 1 protocol ip normal list 102
```

These commands create two priority levels (high and normal) and associate them with ACLs 101 and 102, respectively, allowing high-priority traffic defined in ACL 101 to be transmitted ahead of normal-priority traffic defined in ACL 102.

Furthermore, Class-Based Queuing (CBQ) provides a more flexible approach to traffic prioritization by allowing administrators to define traffic classes based on various criteria such as IP addresses, protocol types, or port numbers. CBQ enables administrators to allocate bandwidth and prioritize traffic based on the requirements of specific applications or users.

To implement CBQ on Cisco routers, administrators can use the Modular QoS CLI (MQC) to define traffic classes and policies. For example, the following commands create a CBQ policy-map that prioritizes VoIP traffic over other traffic types:

pythonCopy code

```
class-map match-all VoIP match ip dscp ef policy-map CBQ class VoIP priority percent 30
```

These commands define a traffic class (VoIP) that matches packets with Expedited Forwarding (EF) DSCP markings and assign a priority of 30% of the interface bandwidth to VoIP traffic in the CBQ policy-map.

In addition to queuing mechanisms, packet marking and classification techniques play a crucial role in QoS prioritization. By marking packets with Differentiated Services Code Point (DSCP) values or Class of Service (CoS) markings, administrators can classify traffic into different priority levels and ensure that network devices prioritize traffic accordingly.

To mark packets with DSCP values, administrators can use the **set dscp** command in a Cisco router's policy-map configuration. For example, the following command marks packets with EF DSCP markings:

arduinoCopy code

```
policy-map QoS class Voice set dscp ef
```

This command ensures that packets matching the Voice class in the QoS policy-map are marked with EF (Expedited Forwarding) DSCP values, indicating high-priority traffic.

In summary, QoS queue management and prioritization techniques are essential for optimizing network performance and ensuring the efficient utilization of network resources. By implementing queuing mechanisms such as WFQ, PQ, CQ, and CBQ, as well as employing packet marking and classification techniques, administrators can prioritize critical traffic, mitigate congestion, and enhance the overall quality of service provided to users and applications across the network.

Chapter 5: Network Security Best Practices

Defense-in-depth is a fundamental approach to cybersecurity that emphasizes the deployment of multiple layers of security mechanisms to protect an organization's IT infrastructure and data from various threats. This comprehensive strategy acknowledges that no single security measure is foolproof and that a multi-layered approach is essential for effectively mitigating cyber risks and minimizing the impact of potential security incidents.

At the core of the defense-in-depth architecture are several key principles and components, each serving a specific purpose in safeguarding the organization's assets. These components include network security appliances, such as firewalls, intrusion detection/prevention systems (IDS/IPS), and secure web gateways (SWGs), as well as endpoint security solutions like antivirus software, endpoint detection and response (EDR) tools, and endpoint protection platforms (EPPs).

To deploy a defense-in-depth architecture, organizations must first conduct a comprehensive risk assessment to identify potential vulnerabilities and threats to their IT infrastructure. This assessment helps determine the appropriate security controls and measures needed to address specific risks effectively.

Once the risk assessment is complete, organizations can begin implementing security controls across multiple layers of their infrastructure. At the network perimeter, firewalls play a crucial role in filtering incoming and outgoing traffic based on predefined security policies. Firewalls can be configured to block unauthorized access attempts, prevent the spread of malware, and enforce security policies to protect sensitive data.

Intrusion detection and prevention systems (IDS/IPS) complement firewalls by monitoring network traffic for suspicious activity and unauthorized access attempts. IDS sensors analyze network packets in real-time, looking for known attack signatures or anomalous behavior that may indicate a security threat. IPS systems can automatically respond to detected threats by blocking malicious traffic or alerting security administrators for further investigation.

Secure web gateways (SWGs) provide additional protection by inspecting web traffic for malware, phishing attempts, and other malicious content. SWGs can enforce web usage policies, filter out malicious websites, and encrypt sensitive data to prevent eavesdropping and data breaches.

At the endpoint level, organizations deploy various security solutions to protect individual devices such as desktops, laptops, and mobile devices. Antivirus software scans files and programs for known malware signatures and removes or quarantines infected files to prevent further damage. Endpoint detection and response (EDR) tools offer advanced threat detection capabilities by monitoring system activities for signs of compromise and responding to security incidents in real-time.

Endpoint protection platforms (EPPs) integrate antivirus, EDR, and other security features into a single solution, providing centralized management and visibility across all endpoints in the organization's network. EPPs help organizations enforce security policies, detect and respond to threats more effectively, and streamline security operations.

In addition to network and endpoint security controls, organizations also implement security best practices such as access control, encryption, and security awareness training to further strengthen their defense-in-depth strategy. Access control mechanisms limit user privileges and restrict access to sensitive data and resources based on user roles and responsibilities.

Encryption helps protect data in transit and at rest by encoding it in such a way that only authorized parties can access and decrypt it. Security awareness training educates employees about common cyber threats, phishing scams, and social engineering tactics, empowering them to recognize and report potential security incidents.

Overall, a defense-in-depth security architecture is a holistic approach to cybersecurity that combines multiple layers of protection to mitigate risks, detect and respond to threats, and safeguard the organization's assets from cyber attacks. By deploying a diverse array of security controls and measures across their infrastructure, organizations can effectively defend against a wide range of security threats and ensure the integrity, confidentiality, and availability of their IT systems and data. Network Access Control (NAC)

Implementation is a crucial aspect of modern network security, providing organizations with the means to enforce policies and ensure that only authorized devices and users can access their networks. NAC solutions enable organizations to strengthen their security posture by implementing granular access controls, enforcing security policies, and monitoring network activity to detect and respond to potential threats.

To implement NAC effectively, organizations must first define their security policies and requirements. This involves identifying the types of devices and users that should be allowed access to the network, as well as determining the level of access privileges each group should have. Security policies may vary depending on factors such as user roles, device types, and the sensitivity of the data being accessed.

Once the security policies have been defined, organizations can begin deploying NAC solutions to enforce these policies and control access to their networks. One common approach to NAC implementation involves the use of IEEE 802.1X authentication, which provides port-based access control for wired and wireless networks. With 802.1X, devices attempting to connect to the network must first authenticate themselves before they are granted access. This authentication process typically involves the exchange of credentials, such as usernames and passwords, certificates, or other forms of authentication.

To deploy 802.1X authentication, organizations must configure their network devices, such as switches, routers, and wireless access points, to support the protocol. This typically involves enabling 802.1X authentication on network ports and configuring authentication settings, such as the authentication method (e.g., EAP-TLS, EAP-PEAP, EAP-TTLS), authentication server parameters, and access control policies.

For example, to enable 802.1X authentication on a Cisco Catalyst switch port, administrators can use the following CLI commands:

scssCopy code

Switch(config)# interface <interface> Switch(config-if)# dot1x port-control auto Switch(config-if)# dot1x host-mode multi-auth Switch(config-if)# dot1x control-direction in Switch(config-if)# authentication port-control auto Switch(config-if)# exit Switch(config)# aaa new-model Switch(config)# aaa authentication dot1x default group radius Switch(config)# radius-server host <IP_address> key <shared_secret>

In this example, the "dot1x port-control auto" command enables 802.1X port-based authentication on the specified interface, while "dot1x host-mode multi-auth" configures the switch to allow multiple devices to authenticate on the same port. The "aaa authentication dot1x default group radius" command specifies that the switch should use a RADIUS server for authentication, and the "radius-server host" command configures the switch to use the specified RADIUS server for authentication.

In addition to 802.1X authentication, NAC solutions may also incorporate other authentication methods and technologies, such as MAC address filtering, captive portals, and integration with identity and access management (IAM) systems. These additional authentication mechanisms can help organizations enforce security policies and ensure that only authorized devices and users are granted access to the network.

Once NAC solutions are deployed, organizations must regularly monitor and manage their network access controls to ensure ongoing compliance with security policies and regulatory requirements. This includes monitoring network traffic, analyzing authentication logs, and conducting periodic security assessments to identify and address any vulnerabilities or security gaps.

Overall, NAC implementation is a critical component of modern network security, providing organizations with the means to enforce access controls, protect against unauthorized access, and mitigate the risk of security breaches. By implementing NAC solutions and adhering to best practices for configuration and management, organizations can enhance their overall security posture and better protect their networks and sensitive data from cyber threats.

Chapter 6: Advanced Firewall Configuration

Stateful and stateless firewalls are two primary types of network security devices that protect networks by controlling the flow of traffic based on predetermined rules and policies. Understanding the differences between these two types of firewalls is essential for network administrators when designing and implementing effective security measures.

Stateless firewalls, also known as packet-filtering firewalls, examine each individual packet of data passing through the firewall and make decisions based solely on the information contained within that packet, such as source and destination IP addresses, port numbers, and protocol types. Stateless firewalls do not maintain any knowledge of the state of connections or sessions, making their decision-making process based on static rules defined by administrators.

To deploy a stateless firewall, administrators typically configure access control lists (ACLs) on routers or dedicated firewall appliances to allow or deny traffic based on specific criteria. For example, to create an ACL on a Cisco router to permit HTTP traffic from a specific source IP address, administrators can use the following command:

arduinoCopy code

Router(config)# access-list 101 permit tcp <source_IP> 0.0.0.0 eq 80

This command creates an ACL numbered 101 that permits TCP traffic from the specified source IP address to port 80 (HTTP). The ACL can then be applied to an interface to control traffic flow.

Stateful firewalls, on the other hand, maintain knowledge of the state of active connections by tracking the state of each session passing through the firewall. This includes information such as source and destination IP addresses, port numbers, sequence numbers, and connection flags. By maintaining this state information, stateful firewalls can make more informed decisions about whether to allow or deny traffic based on the context of the entire communication session.

To deploy a stateful firewall, administrators typically configure rules that govern the handling of traffic based on the state of connections. For example, to configure a stateful firewall rule on a Palo Alto Networks firewall to allow inbound SSH traffic only if it is part of an established session, administrators can use the following command:

arduinoCopy code

```
PaloAlto(config)# set rulebase security rules <rule_name> from <source_zone> to <destination_zone> source <source_address> destination <destination_address> service ssh action allow
```

This command creates a rule that allows SSH traffic from a specific source address to a specific destination address only if it is part of an established session.

One of the key advantages of stateful firewalls is their ability to provide more granular control over network traffic and better protection against sophisticated threats such as network-based attacks and application-layer attacks. By maintaining state information for each connection, stateful firewalls can identify and block malicious traffic that may attempt to exploit vulnerabilities in network protocols or applications.

In contrast, stateless firewalls are generally simpler and more lightweight than stateful firewalls, making them suitable for environments where basic packet filtering is sufficient or where resources are limited. However, stateless firewalls may be less effective at detecting and blocking certain types of attacks, particularly those that rely on exploiting the stateful nature of network protocols.

Overall, the choice between stateful and stateless firewalls depends on the specific security requirements and operational needs of an organization. While stateful firewalls offer more advanced features and capabilities for protecting against sophisticated threats, stateless firewalls may be more suitable for simple network configurations or environments with limited resources. By understanding the differences between these two types of firewalls, network administrators can make informed decisions about the most appropriate firewall solution for their organization's security needs. Intrusion Detection and Prevention Systems (IDPS) play a crucial role in safeguarding networks and systems against unauthorized access, malicious activities, and potential security breaches. Integrating IDPS into an organization's existing security infrastructure enhances its overall security posture by providing real-time monitoring, detection, and response capabilities to mitigate threats effectively.

The integration of IDPS involves deploying and configuring these systems to work seamlessly with other security components, such as firewalls, antivirus solutions, and security information and event management (SIEM) systems. This ensures comprehensive protection against a wide range of cyber threats and vulnerabilities.

One common approach to IDPS integration is deploying IDPS sensors strategically throughout the network to monitor traffic and detect potential security incidents. These sensors analyze network packets, log events, and generate alerts based on predefined rules and signatures. To deploy IDPS sensors effectively, network administrators need to consider factors such as network topology, traffic patterns, and critical assets to ensure comprehensive coverage and maximum visibility.

For example, deploying IDPS sensors at network ingress and egress points, as well as within internal network segments, allows organizations to monitor traffic entering and exiting the network and detect suspicious activities within their internal infrastructure. Using command-line interfaces (CLI) or management consoles provided by IDPS vendors, administrators can configure sensor settings, define detection rules, and customize alerting thresholds to align with their organization's security policies and requirements.

Once IDPS sensors are deployed, the next step in integration involves correlating and analyzing security events and alerts generated by these sensors with other security data sources. This is where integration with SIEM systems becomes crucial. SIEM platforms aggregate and correlate security events from various sources, including IDPS, firewalls, antivirus solutions, and log files, to provide a unified view of the organization's security posture.

To integrate IDPS with a SIEM system, administrators configure event forwarding or logging settings on the IDPS sensors to send security events and alerts to the SIEM platform for centralized monitoring and analysis. CLI commands or graphical user interfaces (GUIs) provided by both IDPS and SIEM vendors facilitate this integration process, allowing administrators to specify destination addresses, protocols, and authentication credentials for event transmission.

By integrating IDPS with SIEM, organizations can leverage advanced analytics and threat intelligence capabilities to correlate security events, detect patterns of suspicious behavior, and prioritize response efforts more effectively. This integration also enables automated incident response workflows, such as triggering alerts, blocking malicious IP addresses, or quarantining compromised devices, based on predefined rules and playbooks.

Furthermore, IDPS integration extends beyond SIEM to encompass collaboration with other security solutions, such as endpoint detection and response (EDR) systems, threat intelligence platforms, and security orchestration, automation, and response (SOAR) tools. This holistic approach to security integration enables organizations to orchestrate proactive defense measures, share threat intelligence, and streamline incident response processes across their entire security infrastructure.

In addition to integrating IDPS with other security components, organizations must ensure proper configuration and tuning of IDPS policies and rules to minimize false positives, optimize detection accuracy, and prioritize critical alerts effectively. CLI commands or configuration wizards provided by IDPS vendors facilitate this process, allowing administrators to fine-tune rule sets, adjust alert thresholds, and customize response actions based on evolving security requirements and threat landscapes.

Moreover, ongoing monitoring, maintenance, and regular updates are essential to ensure the effectiveness of IDPS integration. Administrators should regularly review security event logs, analyze performance metrics, and apply vendor-supplied patches and signature updates to keep IDPS systems up to date and resilient against emerging threats.

In summary, the integration of Intrusion Detection and Prevention Systems (IDPS) into an organization's security infrastructure is a critical aspect of effective cybersecurity strategy. By deploying IDPS sensors, integrating with SIEM and other security solutions, and fine-tuning policies and rules, organizations can enhance their ability to detect, prevent, and respond to security incidents proactively, thereby reducing the risk of data breaches, financial losses, and reputational damage.

Chapter 7: VPN and Remote Access Solutions

Site-to-Site Virtual Private Network (VPN) configuration is a fundamental aspect of network security architecture, enabling secure communication between geographically distributed networks over the internet. This configuration establishes encrypted tunnels between the network gateways, ensuring confidentiality, integrity, and authenticity of data transmitted between sites.

To configure a Site-to-Site VPN, administrators typically utilize VPN protocols such as IPsec (Internet Protocol Security) or SSL/TLS (Secure Sockets Layer/Transport Layer Security) to establish secure connections between the VPN gateways located at each site. IPsec is a widely adopted protocol suite for VPN implementation due to its robust security features and interoperability with various network devices and vendors.

The first step in configuring a Site-to-Site VPN is to determine the VPN topology and identify the network gateways that will serve as VPN endpoints. Administrators need to ensure that these gateways support IPsec VPN functionality and have adequate computational resources to handle encryption and decryption tasks efficiently.

Once the gateways are selected, administrators access their configuration interfaces, which may be command-line interfaces (CLI) or web-based graphical user interfaces (GUI), depending on the device vendor and model. Using the CLI, administrators can enter configuration commands directly into the device's terminal interface to configure VPN settings.

For example, on Cisco routers, administrators can use commands such as "crypto isakmp policy" to define the ISAKMP (Internet Security Association and Key Management Protocol) policy parameters, including encryption algorithms, authentication methods, and key exchange protocols. Similarly, the "crypto ipsec transform-set" command is used to specify the IPsec transform sets, which define the encryption and authentication algorithms used to protect VPN traffic.

After configuring the ISAKMP policy and IPsec transform sets, administrators define the VPN peer configurations, including peer IP addresses, pre-shared keys or digital certificates for authentication, and access control lists (ACLs) to specify permitted traffic between sites. The "crypto map" command is commonly used to create crypto maps, which define the VPN policies and associate them with specific interfaces and traffic flows.

For example, administrators can use the "crypto map" command to create a crypto map named "VPN_MAP" and apply it to the outside interface of the VPN gateway. Within the crypto map configuration, administrators specify the peer IP address, transform set, and ACL defining the interesting traffic to be encrypted and transmitted over the VPN tunnel.

Once the VPN configurations are applied to both VPN gateways, the devices establish a secure VPN tunnel between them, encrypting and encapsulating the data traffic according to the defined policies. Administrators can use monitoring tools and CLI commands such as "show crypto isakmp sa" and "show crypto ipsec sa" to verify the status of VPN tunnels, monitor traffic statistics, and troubleshoot connectivity issues.

In addition to IPsec, administrators may choose to configure Site-to-Site VPNs using SSL/TLS VPN protocols, which offer advantages such as ease of deployment, support for web-based applications, and compatibility with devices that do not support IPsec. SSL/TLS VPN configurations typically involve configuring VPN profiles, defining access control policies, and configuring SSL certificate authentication.

For example, in a Cisco ASA (Adaptive Security Appliance) firewall, administrators can use the ASDM (Adaptive Security Device Manager) GUI to create SSL VPN profiles, define user authentication methods, and configure access control policies based on user roles and groups. CLI commands such as "ssl trust-point" are used to specify SSL certificates for client and server authentication.

Once the SSL VPN configuration is applied, remote users can establish secure VPN connections to the corporate network using SSL VPN client software or web browsers, providing secure access to internal resources and applications from any location with internet connectivity.

In summary, configuring Site-to-Site VPNs involves defining VPN policies, configuring encryption parameters, specifying authentication methods, and establishing secure tunnels between VPN gateways. Whether using IPsec or SSL/TLS VPN protocols, administrators must carefully plan and deploy VPN configurations to ensure secure and reliable communication between geographically distributed networks. Regular monitoring and maintenance are essential to ensure the continued effectiveness and security of Site-to-Site VPN deployments.

Remote Access Virtual Private Network (VPN) deployment strategies play a crucial role in enabling secure remote connectivity for users accessing corporate resources from external locations. Remote Access VPNs establish encrypted tunnels between remote users and the corporate network, ensuring data confidentiality, integrity, and authentication.

One common deployment strategy for Remote Access VPNs is the use of client-based VPN solutions, where remote users install VPN client software on their devices to establish secure connections to the corporate network. VPN client software is available for various operating systems, including Windows, macOS, Linux, iOS, and Android, providing flexibility for users with different device types.

To deploy client-based Remote Access VPNs, administrators configure VPN server settings on the corporate network gateway or firewall device. They define VPN user profiles, authentication methods, encryption algorithms, and access control policies to govern remote user access to internal resources.

For example, on a Cisco ASA firewall, administrators use the ASDM GUI or CLI commands to configure VPN group policies, which specify parameters such as VPN group names, authentication methods (e.g., pre-shared keys, digital certificates), encryption algorithms, and split-tunneling policies. Split-tunneling allows remote users to access both corporate and internet resources simultaneously while connected to the VPN.

Once the VPN server settings are configured, administrators distribute VPN client software to remote users, along with instructions for configuring VPN client profiles. Users install the VPN client software on their devices and configure VPN connection profiles with the server's IP address or hostname, authentication credentials, and other parameters specified by the administrator.

Upon establishing a VPN connection, the client-based VPN software encrypts all network traffic between the remote user's device and the corporate network gateway, ensuring secure communication over untrusted networks such as the internet. Administrators can monitor VPN connections and manage user access through centralized VPN management consoles or monitoring tools.

Another deployment strategy for Remote Access VPNs is the use of browser-based SSL VPN solutions, which allow remote users to access corporate resources securely through web browsers without requiring VPN client software installation. SSL VPN solutions leverage HTTPS (Hypertext Transfer Protocol Secure) for encrypted communication between the remote user's browser and the SSL VPN gateway.

To deploy SSL VPNs, administrators configure SSL VPN gateway settings on dedicated appliances or integrated security devices such as firewalls or application delivery controllers. They define SSL VPN user authentication methods, access control policies, and resource access rules to govern remote user access to internal web applications, file shares, and other resources.

For example, on a Palo Alto Networks firewall, administrators use the web-based management interface to configure SSL VPN settings, including SSL/TLS certificate authentication, user authentication profiles (e.g., LDAP,

RADIUS), and clientless VPN portal configurations. Clientless VPN portals provide remote users with web-based access to internal resources through a secure web portal interface.

Once the SSL VPN gateway settings are configured, remote users access the SSL VPN portal URL using a web browser and authenticate themselves using their credentials. Upon successful authentication, users can access authorized resources through the SSL VPN portal, which provides a user-friendly interface for accessing web applications, file shares, and intranet sites.

SSL VPN solutions offer advantages such as ease of deployment, compatibility with any device with a web browser, and granular access control based on user roles and permissions. However, they may have limitations in supporting non-web-based applications and require additional configuration for full network-level access.

In summary, Remote Access VPN deployment strategies involve configuring VPN server settings, defining user authentication methods, distributing VPN client software (for client-based VPNs), and configuring access control policies to govern remote user access to corporate resources. Whether deploying client-based VPNs or browser-based SSL VPNs, administrators must consider factors such as security requirements, user convenience, and scalability to ensure effective and secure remote connectivity for users accessing corporate networks from external locations. Regular monitoring and maintenance are essential to ensure the continued security and reliability of Remote Access VPN deployments.

Chapter 8: Network Design and Optimization Strategies

Hierarchical network design principles form the foundation for building scalable, efficient, and manageable networks by organizing network devices into logical layers that serve specific functions and responsibilities. These principles guide network architects and administrators in designing networks that meet current requirements while allowing for future growth and adaptability to evolving technologies and business needs.

At the core of hierarchical network design is the concept of dividing network infrastructure into distinct layers, each serving a specific purpose and providing defined services. This approach simplifies network management, enhances performance, and facilitates troubleshooting by compartmentalizing network functions and reducing complexity.

One fundamental aspect of hierarchical network design is the division of network devices into three primary layers: the core layer, distribution layer, and access layer. Each layer plays a critical role in facilitating communication within the network and between different network segments.

Starting with the core layer, it serves as the backbone of the network, responsible for high-speed, reliable packet forwarding between different parts of the network. The core layer typically consists of high-performance switches and routers optimized for fast packet switching and minimal latency. CLI commands such as configuring routing protocols like OSPF or BGP and setting up VLANs using commands like **vlan create** and **vlan assign** are commonly used at this layer to ensure efficient routing and traffic forwarding.

Moving outward, the distribution layer acts as an intermediary between the core and access layers, providing aggregation and distribution of network traffic. This layer performs functions such as VLAN segmentation, access control, and policy enforcement. CLI commands like **interface trunk** for configuring trunk links between switches and **ip access-list** for implementing access control lists (ACLs) are essential for configuring the distribution layer to manage traffic flow effectively.

Finally, the access layer connects end-user devices such as computers, printers, and IP phones to the network infrastructure. This layer provides connectivity to individual devices and enforces network policies at the point of entry into the network. CLI commands like **interface range** for configuring multiple interfaces simultaneously and **switchport access** for defining access ports are commonly used at the access layer to configure connectivity for end devices and enforce security policies.

In addition to the three primary layers, hierarchical network design principles also emphasize modularization and scalability. By breaking down the network into smaller, manageable modules or domains, organizations can simplify network management and accommodate growth without sacrificing performance or reliability.

Modularization allows for the deployment of standardized building blocks or network modules that can be replicated across different parts of the network. This approach simplifies network provisioning and troubleshooting and enables organizations to scale their networks efficiently. CLI commands such as **interface vlan** for creating virtual LAN interfaces and **ip route** for defining static routes are instrumental in configuring modular network designs.

Furthermore, hierarchical network design principles advocate for redundancy and fault tolerance to ensure high availability and resilience. Redundant links, devices, and paths are strategically deployed to provide backup routes and failover mechanisms in case of network failures or outages. CLI commands like **spanning-tree portfast** for enabling rapid spanning tree protocol (RSTP) on access ports and **redundancy protocol** for configuring high-availability protocols such as Hot Standby Router Protocol (HSRP) are essential for implementing redundancy in network designs.

Another key aspect of hierarchical network design is segmentation and isolation of network traffic to enhance security and optimize performance. VLANs are commonly used to segregate traffic into separate broadcast domains, limiting the scope of broadcast storms and enhancing network security. CLI commands like **vlan database** for configuring VLANs and **switchport mode** for defining access or trunk ports are essential for implementing VLAN-based segmentation.

In summary, hierarchical network design principles provide a structured framework for building scalable, efficient, and resilient network infrastructures. By organizing network devices into distinct layers, modularizing network components, implementing redundancy and fault tolerance, and segmenting network traffic, organizations can create robust and manageable networks that meet the demands of modern business environments. CLI commands play a crucial role in configuring and deploying hierarchical network designs, enabling network administrators to implement best practices and optimize network performance and reliability.

Capacity planning and network scaling are crucial aspects of managing network infrastructure to ensure that it can support current and future demands without performance degradation or bottlenecks. This process involves analyzing current network usage patterns, forecasting future requirements, and implementing strategies to scale network resources effectively.

One of the first steps in capacity planning is to gather data on current network usage, including traffic volume, bandwidth utilization, and application requirements. This data can be collected using network monitoring tools such as SNMP (Simple Network Management Protocol) or packet analyzers like Wireshark. By examining this data, network administrators can identify potential areas of congestion or performance bottlenecks that may require additional capacity.

Once current network usage patterns are understood, the next step is to forecast future growth and demand. This involves considering factors such as business expansion, increasing user numbers, and the adoption of new applications or services. Network administrators can use historical data and trend analysis to predict future network requirements and estimate the amount of additional capacity needed to accommodate growth.

Based on these forecasts, network administrators can develop a capacity planning strategy that outlines how to scale network resources to meet future demand. This strategy may include upgrading hardware components such as routers, switches, and firewalls to support higher bandwidth requirements, adding additional network links to increase capacity, or optimizing network configuration settings to improve performance.

CLI commands play a vital role in implementing capacity planning strategies, as they allow network administrators to configure and manage network devices efficiently. For example, when upgrading network hardware, commands such as **interface** for configuring interfaces, **ip route** for defining routing tables, and **vlan** for creating VLANs are commonly used. Similarly, when adding new network links, commands like **interface port-channel** for configuring port-channel interfaces and **spanning-tree** for configuring spanning tree protocol settings may be used.

In addition to upgrading hardware components, network scaling may also involve optimizing network design and configuration to improve efficiency and performance. This could include implementing techniques such as traffic engineering to dynamically route traffic based on network conditions or deploying Quality of Service (QoS) policies to prioritize critical traffic types.

CLI commands are essential for implementing these optimization techniques. For example, commands like **ip route** with traffic engineering extensions can be used to configure traffic engineering policies, while commands like **class-map** and **policy-map** are used to define QoS policies. By fine-tuning network configuration settings, administrators can optimize network performance and ensure that critical applications receive the necessary bandwidth and resources. Another aspect of capacity planning and network scaling is evaluating the scalability of network architecture and identifying potential limitations or constraints. This involves assessing factors such as the scalability of routing protocols, the capacity of network devices, and the effectiveness of network management tools.

CLI commands can be used to assess the scalability of network components and identify potential bottlenecks. For example, commands like **show ip route** and **show ip bgp** can be used to examine routing tables and identify any scalability issues with routing protocols. Similarly, commands like **show interface** can be used to monitor interface utilization and identify any interfaces that may be approaching capacity.

Once potential scalability issues have been identified, network administrators can take steps to address them, such as upgrading hardware components, optimizing routing protocols, or redesigning network architecture. CLI commands are instrumental in implementing these changes and ensuring that the network can scale effectively to meet future demand.

In summary, capacity planning and network scaling are essential processes for ensuring that network infrastructure can support current and future demands effectively. By analyzing current network usage, forecasting future requirements, and implementing strategies to scale network resources, organizations can ensure that their networks remain reliable, efficient, and capable of meeting the needs of users and applications. CLI commands play a critical role in implementing capacity planning strategies, allowing network administrators to configure and manage network devices efficiently and optimize network performance and scalability.

Chapter 9: Cloud Networking and SDN Fundamentals

Cloud deployment models refer to different approaches for deploying and managing cloud computing resources, each offering unique benefits and considerations. Understanding these deployment models is crucial for organizations seeking to leverage cloud services effectively.

One of the most common cloud deployment models is the public cloud, where cloud services and resources are provided by third-party service providers over the internet. Organizations can access and utilize these resources on a pay-as-you-go basis, making it a cost-effective option for businesses of all sizes. Popular public cloud providers include Amazon Web Services (AWS), Microsoft Azure, and Google Cloud Platform (GCP).

To deploy resources in a public cloud environment, organizations typically use the provider's management console or command-line interface (CLI) tools. For example, AWS provides the AWS Management Console and AWS Command Line Interface (CLI) for managing cloud resources. Users can use commands such as **aws ec2 create-instance** to provision virtual machines or **aws s3 cp** to copy files to Amazon Simple Storage Service (S3).

Another cloud deployment model is the private cloud, where cloud infrastructure is dedicated solely to a single organization. This model offers greater control, security, and customization options compared to public cloud environments. Organizations can deploy a private cloud infrastructure on-premises using their hardware and software resources or opt for a hosted private cloud solution provided by a third-party vendor.

Deploying a private cloud typically involves setting up virtualization technology such as VMware vSphere or Microsoft Hyper-V to create virtualized infrastructure. Administrators can then use management tools like VMware vCenter or Microsoft System Center to provision and manage virtual machines. CLI commands such as **vmware-cmd** or **Get-VM** in PowerShell can be used to manage virtual machines and perform tasks such as creating snapshots or resizing virtual disks.

Hybrid cloud is another deployment model that combines elements of both public and private clouds. In a hybrid cloud environment, organizations can use a mix of on-premises infrastructure, private cloud resources, and public cloud services to meet their specific needs. This model offers flexibility, allowing organizations to leverage the scalability and cost-effectiveness of public cloud services while maintaining control over sensitive data and critical workloads in a private cloud environment.

Deploying and managing a hybrid cloud environment requires integration between on-premises infrastructure and public cloud services. Organizations can use tools like AWS Direct Connect or Azure ExpressRoute to establish dedicated network connections between their on-premises data centers and public cloud regions. CLI commands such as **aws directconnect create-connection** or **New-AzureDedicatedCircuit** can be used to create these connections.

A related deployment model is the multi-cloud, where organizations utilize services and resources from multiple cloud providers simultaneously. This approach offers redundancy, resilience, and flexibility, allowing organizations to avoid vendor lock-in and choose the best-of-breed solutions for their specific requirements.

Managing a multi-cloud environment involves coordinating resources and services across different cloud platforms. Organizations can use cloud management platforms (CMPs) or cloud orchestration tools to streamline provisioning, monitoring, and governance tasks. CLI commands such as **terraform apply** or **kubectl apply** can be used to deploy and manage infrastructure as code (IaC) or containerized workloads across multiple cloud environments.

Finally, there is the community cloud deployment model, where cloud infrastructure is shared by several organizations with similar interests, such as government agencies or research institutions. This model offers cost-sharing benefits and enables collaboration and resource pooling among community members.

Deploying resources in a community cloud typically involves adhering to specific compliance and security requirements established by the community members. Organizations may use custom-built solutions or specialized cloud providers catering to the needs of the community. CLI commands similar to those used in public or private clouds can be utilized, depending on the underlying infrastructure and management tools available.

In summary, understanding the different cloud deployment models is essential for organizations looking to leverage cloud computing effectively. Whether deploying resources in a public, private, hybrid, multi-cloud, or community cloud environment, organizations must consider factors such as scalability, security, compliance, and cost to meet their specific business requirements. By choosing the right deployment model and leveraging appropriate management tools and CLI commands, organizations can unlock the full potential of cloud computing and drive innovation and growth. Software-Defined Networking (SDN) architecture represents a fundamental shift in how networks are designed, deployed, and managed, offering greater flexibility, agility, and automation. At its core, SDN decouples the control plane from the data plane, enabling centralized management and programmability of network devices.

In an SDN architecture, the control plane, responsible for making forwarding decisions, is abstracted from the physical network devices such as switches and routers. Instead, a centralized controller, often implemented as software running on commodity hardware, orchestrates the behavior of network devices based on high-level policies and rules.

One of the key components of an SDN architecture is the SDN controller, which serves as the brain of the network, providing a centralized point of control and management. Examples of popular SDN controllers include OpenDaylight, ONOS, and Ryu.

To deploy an SDN controller, organizations can download the software package from the respective project website and install it on a server or virtual machine. For instance, to install OpenDaylight, users can download the distribution package and run the installation command such as **sudo apt-get install opendaylight** on a Linux-based system.

Once the SDN controller is installed, administrators can use its web-based interface or RESTful APIs to define network policies, configure routing behavior, and monitor network traffic. For example, in OpenDaylight, administrators can define flow rules using the OpenFlow protocol to control packet forwarding behavior in the network.

Another essential component of an SDN architecture is the southbound interface, which enables communication between the SDN controller and network devices at the data plane. The most widely used southbound protocol in SDN is OpenFlow, an open standard that allows the controller to communicate with switches and routers to program their forwarding tables.

To enable OpenFlow on network switches, administrators must configure them to operate in OpenFlow mode and establish a connection with the SDN controller. This can be done using CLI commands specific to the switch vendor. For example, on a Cisco switch, administrators can use commands such as **feature sdn** to enable OpenFlow support.

In addition to the control and data planes, SDN architectures often incorporate a northbound interface, which provides a way for higher-level applications and services to interact with the SDN controller. The northbound interface abstracts the underlying network complexity and exposes a set of APIs that developers can use to create custom network applications and services.

Developers can use these APIs to build applications that leverage the programmability of the SDN controller to implement advanced network functionality. For example, an application could dynamically adjust network bandwidth based on application demand or automatically reroute traffic in response to network congestion.

To develop applications that interact with an SDN controller's northbound interface, developers typically use programming languages such as Python or Java and SDKs provided by the controller vendor. For example, the OpenDaylight controller provides a Java-based SDK that developers can use to build custom applications.

SDN architectures also support the concept of network virtualization, allowing multiple logical networks to coexist on the same physical infrastructure. Network virtualization enables organizations to create isolated network segments, or virtual networks, with their own addressing, routing, and security policies.

To deploy network virtualization in an SDN architecture, administrators can use technologies such as Virtual Extensible LAN (VXLAN) or Generic Routing Encapsulation (GRE) to encapsulate traffic from different virtual networks and overlay them on the physical network infrastructure. This allows for greater flexibility and scalability in network design and deployment.

Overall, Software-Defined Networking (SDN) architecture represents a paradigm shift in network design and management, offering centralized control, programmability, and automation. By decoupling the control plane from the data plane and providing open interfaces for customization and integration, SDN enables organizations to build more agile, efficient, and scalable networks that can adapt to evolving business requirements.

Chapter 10: Troubleshooting Scalability and Performance Issues

Performance monitoring tools play a critical role in ensuring the optimal operation and scalability of IT infrastructure. These tools provide insights into the performance metrics of various components within a system, helping administrators identify bottlenecks, diagnose issues, and optimize resource utilization. By continuously monitoring key performance indicators (KPIs), organizations can proactively address performance issues, improve efficiency, and enhance the overall user experience.

One of the widely used performance monitoring tools is Nagios, an open-source monitoring solution known for its flexibility and extensibility. Nagios allows administrators to monitor the availability, performance, and status of network services, servers, and applications in real-time. Using Nagios, administrators can configure checks for various metrics such as CPU usage, memory utilization, disk space, and network traffic. They can also define thresholds and alerts to be notified of any deviations from normal operating conditions.

To deploy Nagios, administrators can download the software package from the official website and install it on a dedicated server or virtual machine. Once installed, they can configure Nagios to monitor the desired resources by defining hosts, services, and checks using configuration files. For example, to monitor the CPU usage of a server, administrators can define a service check using the **check_cpu** command in the Nagios configuration file.

Another popular performance monitoring tool is Zabbix, an enterprise-class open-source monitoring solution known for its scalability and robustness. Zabbix provides a centralized platform for monitoring the performance of servers, network devices, databases, and applications. It offers a wide range of monitoring capabilities, including agent-based and agentless monitoring, SNMP monitoring, and custom script execution.

To deploy Zabbix, administrators can download the software package from the official website and install it on a server or virtual machine. After installation, they can configure Zabbix to monitor the desired resources by adding hosts and defining items, triggers, and actions. For example, to monitor the network bandwidth of a router, administrators can configure an SNMP item to query the router's interface statistics periodically.

Prometheus is another popular performance monitoring tool widely used in cloud-native environments and containerized applications. Prometheus is an open-source monitoring and alerting toolkit designed for reliability, scalability, and ease of use. It collects time-series data from various targets using a pull-based model and stores it in a multi-dimensional data model. Prometheus offers powerful querying capabilities and built-in support for visualization and alerting.

To deploy Prometheus, administrators can download the software package from the official website and install it on a server or containerized environment. They can then configure Prometheus to scrape metrics from the desired targets by defining scrape configurations in the

prometheus.yml configuration file. For example, to monitor the CPU usage of a containerized application, administrators can configure Prometheus to scrape metrics from the application's **/metrics** endpoint.

In addition to these open-source solutions, there are also commercial performance monitoring tools available in the market, such as SolarWinds Orion, Dynatrace, and AppDynamics. These tools offer advanced features and capabilities, including automatic discovery, deep dive diagnostics, and predictive analytics. While commercial solutions often come with licensing fees, they may provide additional value in terms of ease of use, scalability, and support.

Regardless of the specific performance monitoring tool chosen, it is essential to define a comprehensive monitoring strategy that aligns with the organization's goals and requirements. This includes identifying key performance metrics, defining monitoring thresholds and alerts, configuring dashboards and reports, and establishing processes for incident response and resolution.

By leveraging performance monitoring tools effectively, organizations can gain valuable insights into the health and performance of their IT infrastructure, identify areas for improvement, and ensure the scalability and reliability of their systems and applications.

Root cause analysis (RCA) is a systematic process used to identify the underlying reasons or root causes of performance degradation in a system or application. It is a crucial step in troubleshooting and problem-solving, aiming to address the fundamental issues rather than just treating the symptoms. In complex IT environments, performance degradation can arise from various factors, including hardware failures, software bugs, configuration errors, resource contention, network issues, and external dependencies.

To conduct root cause analysis effectively, IT professionals often employ a combination of techniques, tools, and methodologies to systematically investigate and diagnose the problem. One common approach is to follow a structured methodology, such as the "5 Whys" technique or the Fishbone diagram (also known as the Ishikawa diagram), to dig deeper into the underlying causes of the performance issue.

The "5 Whys" technique involves asking a series of "why" questions to uncover the root cause of a problem. By repeatedly asking "why" and drilling down to successive layers of causality, practitioners can trace the problem back to its origin. For example, if an application is experiencing slow response times, the first "why" question might be "Why is the application responding slowly?" The subsequent answers lead to further questions until the root cause is identified.

Similarly, the Fishbone diagram is a visual tool that helps identify potential causes of a problem by categorizing them into different factors, such as people, processes, equipment, environment, and management. Each category serves as a branch on the diagram, with potential causes listed underneath. This method allows teams to brainstorm and analyze the possible causes collaboratively.

In addition to these techniques, performance monitoring tools play a critical role in root cause analysis by providing insights into system behavior, resource utilization, and performance metrics. These tools collect and analyze data from various sources, such as servers, applications, databases, network devices, and infrastructure components, to identify anomalies and performance bottlenecks.

One commonly used performance monitoring tool is Nagios, an open-source monitoring system that helps IT teams identify and resolve infrastructure problems before they affect critical business processes. Nagios allows administrators to monitor network services, host resources, and environmental factors, such as temperature and humidity, using plugins and extensions.

To deploy Nagios, administrators can install it on a Linux-based server using package management tools such as apt or yum. After installation, they can configure monitoring checks for specific services and devices using configuration files or the web-based interface. For example, to monitor the availability of a web server, administrators can use the **check_http** plugin to send HTTP requests and check for a valid response.

Another widely used performance monitoring tool is Zabbix, which offers similar functionality to Nagios but with additional features such as real-time monitoring, auto-discovery, and trend prediction. Zabbix uses agents installed on monitored hosts to collect data on system performance, network traffic, and application behavior, allowing administrators to visualize and analyze performance metrics through a web-based dashboard.

To deploy Zabbix, administrators can download the installation package from the official website and follow the installation instructions for their operating system.

Once installed, they can configure monitoring templates, triggers, and notifications to alert them of performance issues or anomalies.

In addition to these open-source tools, commercial performance monitoring solutions such as SolarWinds Orion, Dynatrace, and New Relic offer advanced features for root cause analysis, including application tracing, log analysis, and distributed tracing. These tools provide comprehensive insights into application performance across distributed environments, helping organizations identify and resolve performance issues quickly.

When conducting root cause analysis, it's essential to gather as much relevant data as possible to understand the context of the problem and its impact on the system. This may involve collecting log files, system metrics, network traces, and configuration settings from various sources to correlate events and identify patterns.

Once the root cause of the performance degradation is identified, IT teams can take corrective actions to address the issue and prevent recurrence. This may involve applying software patches, adjusting configuration settings, reallocating resources, upgrading hardware components, or optimizing application code.

In summary, root cause analysis is a critical process for diagnosing and resolving performance degradation in IT systems and applications. By following structured methodologies, leveraging performance monitoring tools, and collecting relevant data, organizations can uncover the underlying causes of performance issues and implement effective solutions to improve system reliability, availability, and performance.

Conclusion

In summary, the "Desktop Support Crash Course: Technical Problem Solving And Network Troubleshooting" bundle offers a comprehensive and structured approach to mastering the essential skills required for desktop support professionals. Through the four books included in this bundle, readers are guided from the fundamentals of troubleshooting desktop issues to advanced strategies for diagnosing and resolving complex network problems.

Book 1, "Desktop Support Essentials: A Beginner's Guide to Troubleshooting," serves as an entry point for newcomers to the field, providing a solid foundation in desktop support principles and techniques. Readers learn how to identify common hardware and software issues, troubleshoot operating system problems, and effectively communicate with end-users.

Building on this foundation, Book 2, "Mastering Network Basics: Fundamental Techniques for Desktop Support," delves into the fundamentals of networking, equipping readers with the knowledge and skills needed to troubleshoot basic network connectivity issues. From understanding IP addressing and subnetting to configuring network devices and protocols, this book provides a solid understanding of network fundamentals essential for desktop support professionals.

Book 3, "Advanced Desktop Support Strategies: Deep Dive into System Diagnostics," takes readers to the next level by exploring advanced troubleshooting techniques and system diagnostics. Readers learn how to analyze system logs, perform performance tuning, and troubleshoot complex hardware and software issues. With practical examples and case studies, this book prepares readers to tackle challenging desktop support scenarios with confidence.

Finally, Book 4, "Expert-Level Network Troubleshooting: Pro Tips for Resolving Complex Issues," focuses on advanced network troubleshooting strategies and techniques. Readers delve into topics such as packet analysis, protocol analysis, and network security, gaining insights into diagnosing and resolving complex network issues efficiently. With real-world scenarios and expert tips, this book empowers readers to tackle even the most challenging network problems.

Together, the four books in the "Desktop Support Crash Course" bundle offer a comprehensive learning experience that covers the entire spectrum of desktop support and network troubleshooting. Whether you're new to the field or a seasoned professional looking to enhance your skills, this bundle provides the knowledge, tools, and techniques needed to excel in desktop support and network troubleshooting roles.